ABOUT THE IAN

"When the wealthy and v[...] ney put on their finest tailored cocktail wear, uncork the vintage wine, open the box of good cigars—and put in a call to Steve Cohen."

—*Smoke* magazine

"Steve Cohen's elegant and enchanting show will take you 'out of the box' of habitual perception. More than just entertainment, Cohen offers a master class in presentation skills, timing, and awareness."

—Michael Gelb, author of
How to Think Like Leonardo da Vinci

"Some of the smoothest, cleverest, funniest, most baffling magic you'll ever see. Steve Cohen is one of the real originals."

—Kenneth Silverman, Pulitzer Prize—
winning biographer of Harry Houdini

"A heart-stopping act."

—*New York Times*

"A magic show for people who don't like magic shows."

—Jeannie Moos, CNN

"Steve Cohen is one of the most remarkable mindreaders and conjurors in the world. Now I know what rich and powerful people obsessed with controlling their own lives will pay so much for: the existence of the inexplicable."

—*The Independent* (London)

"Bravo to a true virtuoso."

—Sir André Previn, conductor

ABOUT WIN THE CROWD

"If you think magic is just about tricks, you probably think business success is about nothing but spreadsheets and long hours. At long last, Steve Cohen reveals the secrets of both. No sleight of hand, just practical miracles!"

—Seth Godin, author of *Purple Cow*

"The secrets in *Win the Crowd* have helped me capture some of the toughest crowds of all—hard-core businesspeople. I now have the ability to convey my message in a powerful way to both large and small audiences, and you can learn how to do it too."

—Stephen Messer, CEO and chairman, LinkShare Corporation

"*Win the Crowd* is worth its weight in gold if you want to learn the real secret of magicians—showmanship."

—Alan Greenberg, Chairman of the Executive Committee,
The Bear Stearns Companies Inc.

"This book is outstanding. I love the insights into human nature, the stories, the writing style, and the sense of power it helps readers awaken in themselves. This is a real surprise and a true masterpiece."

—Joe Vitale, author of *The Attractor Factor*

WIN

the

CROWD

WIN
the
CROWD

UNLOCK THE SECRETS OF INFLUENCE,
CHARISMA, AND SHOWMANSHIP

STEVE COHEN
The Millionaires' Magician

 Collins
An Imprint of HarperCollinsPublishers

HarperCollins books may be purchased for educational, business, or sales promotional use. For information please write: Special Markets Department, HarperCollins Publishers, 10 East 53rd Street, New York, NY 10022.

FIRST COLLINS EDITION PUBLISHED 2006.

Designed by Nicola Ferguson
Illustrations by Tony Dunn

The Library of Congress has catalogued the hardcover edition as follows:

Cohen, Steve.
     Win the crowd : unlock the secrets of influence, charisma,
and showmanship / Steve Cohen.—1st ed.
          p.   cm.
     ISBN 0-06-074204-6 (hc)
          1. Persuasion (Psychology)   2. Influence (Psychology)   I. Title.

BF637.P4C64   2005
153.8'52—dc22

                                                          2004059762

ISBN-13: 978-0-06-074205-8 (pb)
ISBN-10: 0-06-074205-4 (pb)

06 07 08 09 10 ❖/RRD 10 9 8 7 6 5 4 3 2 1

In memory of my dear friend
magician Mark Nathan Sicher,
who taught me:

"It's not what you do, or how you do it. It's *who* does it.
If they like *you* . . . if the *who* is right . . .
the what and the how *must* be right."

CONTENTS

FOREWORD

STEVE COHEN KNOWS HOW to make things happen and how to get what he wants. The most surprising thing about Steve is that he makes you *want* to help him, and you actually enjoy being influenced by him. His approach is subtle, consistent, and persuasive. People always feel better when they are being sold to if the approach of the salesperson fits in their comfort zone. Steve is a master of this, and it is no accident.

In the time I have known him, I've become a true admirer of his work as well as a friend. His magic is very sophisticated and can be possible only with a very disciplined mind and a strong commitment to his art. He has been a student of human nature ever since his uncle shared some of Houdini's secrets with him.

Steve calls himself a magician, but he is actually a salesperson. What he sells is the enjoyment of wondering how he does what he does. The best salesperson will tell you that they do not want someone to buy from them one time, and they do not want to sell ice to Eskimos. They want to uncover a need, fill it, and have the customer walk away pleased with the purchase. Then they have made a customer for life.

This is what Steve hopes to accomplish with this book. The world always needs great salespeople, and I have no doubt that this book will help anyone who reads it and implements its practices. I know a great salesperson when I see one, and Steve is one of the best. We can all learn a few tricks from him.

Matthew L. Martinucci,
Director of Sales and Marketing,
The Ritz-Carlton, San Francisco

INTRODUCTION

AS a professional magician, I've spent my life collecting, cataloging, and guarding secrets.

The secrets I hold dear are rather esoteric; for instance, how to control the flip of a coin, make metal objects pass through one another, and float a person in thin air. Very intriguing stuff indeed. But in the following pages, I won't be revealing these mechanical or optical secrets. It's not that kind of book.

Instead, I will teach you the psychological principles that make magic work, and how you can use them to win the crowd, whether that crowd consists of one person or hundreds. When you "win the crowd," you win over their hearts in a subtle, nonthreatening way. People won't feel forced or manipulated. The aim is to present yourself with peak levels of confidence and charisma so that audiences are eager to listen to your suggestions, consider your advice, and take action on your words.

As you can imagine, magic is more than just quickness of the hands. It is essentially a mental game of cat-and-mouse, a power play between two minds.

In this book, you will gain access to some highly guarded psychological secrets that no magician has ever released before. Once you learn these secrets, you will want to start using them right away in your daily interactions with other people. You'll discover how to command a room, read people, and build anticipation to a feverish pitch so people are burning to hear what you have to say.

So please, don't keep this book on your desk or coffee table, where others might pick it up and start browsing. Hide it. Guard it from others. After you've finished reading this book, slide it into your bookshelf with the spine pointing inward. If you let other people in on what you are about to learn, the techniques themselves will stop being effective. To gain the greatest results for the time you invest, please agree to keep the contents of this book out of the hands of the merely curious.

WHY DID I WRITE THIS BOOK?

Win the Crowd grew out of constant questioning by my guests at *Chamber Magic*, my weekly show at The Waldorf Towers hotel in New York. After every performance, people would invariably come up to me and ask two questions. First, "Can you make my wife disappear?" And second, "Do these abilities only work here onstage, or can you actually use them in your daily life?"

My pat answer to the first question is, "I have friends in the mob who can make *anyone* disappear for a price!" The answer to the second question, however, is not a joke at all. After sitting through a carefully crafted performance, people recognize that there is something to be learned, something that can be extrapolated for use outside of the entertainment environment.

Personally, I use these human influence techniques both onstage and off. In this book, you'll learn techniques you can use to win any audience. I use the word "audience," but that also includes an audience of one, such as your boss, colleague, or customer.

WHO AM I?

You may have never seen me perform or even heard of me. Although I am in show business, I've intentionally kept a low profile. I make my living by entertaining celebrities, tycoons, and socialites. My clients fly me around the world on private jets to perform for groups of friends and business associates.

Four years ago, I launched a weekly magic show in New York City. The high ticket price meant that I found myself surrounded by millionaires. After seeing the show, many of these clients later invite me to perform strolling entertainment at their own parties. In this very personal and interactive format, I must blend in with the other guests and break the ice during the cocktail hour so that the event kicks off with a jovial atmosphere. I dress in the same type of clothing as the guests and walk among the group without any fanfare or grand introduction. I walk up to a small gathering of socialites, enter into their conversations, and add some witty comments. After they have accepted me, I explain that I have been invited to entertain them and I begin a private performance just inches from their eyes.

The skills that I use to break down barriers and win over a group of skeptical strangers are not specific to magicians. I have discovered some recipes for personal interaction that clearly work if you happen to be a magician; but they have broad applications for everyone else too. In fact, if you are a businessperson, you will likely find that you can incorporate some of these recipes right away to become more confident and persuasive in your daily contact with customers.

WHAT YOU'LL LEARN IN THIS BOOK

Win the Crowd will teach you how to think like a magician. When you strip away the sleight-of-hand tricks, magicians are masters at attracting interest, holding attention, and leaving audiences with fond memories of their time together. Aren't these skills that we can all use? You'll be able to use them after reading this book.

You may be thinking, "But I have no need to impress large auditoriums." That's fine. In addition to learning how to present yourself in front of groups, you'll also learn techniques that'll help you win small, one-on-one personal victories. After all, audiences consist of individuals. Once you know how to convert one skeptic into a supporter, you'll be well prepared for doing the same with groups of skeptics later on.

Most people know the classic magician's rules "Never repeat a trick" and "Never reveal the secret." I've designated five more rules—the Maxims of Magic—that may change the way you interact with people. These maxims will help you wipe out any insecurity you may feel when presenting your ideas to others. These are the rules I live by, both onstage and off.

The Maxims of Magic will help you develop confidence, so you'll always feel in control. Once you read the maxims and apply what you've read, you'll be able to influence others the way that magicians do—through advance preparation and with respect for the audience's intelligence.

Although we magicians deceive people in our shows, deception is not the focus of this book. Rather, you'll learn how to influence people to follow your lead. Audiences do what I ask them to do because they like me. They sense my confidence and assume that I wouldn't waste their time with something not worthwhile. This book teaches you how to position yourself as such a leader and how to refine your own charisma so that people will willingly follow you.

Once you learn how to lead people, you'll need to learn to read them too. After studying this book, you'll know how to relax your mind and body, as I do before every performance. I've included my personal regimen of relaxation exercises, including manipulations of acupressure points and deep breathing techniques. With practice, you will increase your awareness of the thoughts that other people send out to you silently.

Every magician uses magic words, and you'll learn many of them in this book. Chapter 10, "Magic Words," will teach you more than just "abracadabra" and "hocus-pocus." You'll learn how specific word choices can influence the outcome of your verbal interactions with others. Once you've gained authority, these word patterns and turns of phrase will help you keep it. You can easily slip Magic Words into your daily interactions to bolster your powers of persuasion. The chapter is designed just like a foreign language phrase book: you can open to any page and learn how to use a particular word pattern. I've included many examples so that you can see how easy it is to apply these patterns to your life. People will begin to respond predictably—the way that *you* want them to.

Finally, you'll learn about misdirection, the foundation of all physical magic. I almost didn't include this chapter because the material was too good to share, but decided to add it at the last minute. You'll learn how to pinpoint people's attention at all times as you speak, so that they see what you want them to see and ignore everything else.

The best part about the material in this book is that it doesn't require superintelligence or superskill. As long as you have at least average abilities and the desire to improve, you will expand your repertoire of personal influence skills.

Please come to New York and see how I actually use the techniques in these pages in my live performances of *Chamber Magic*. If you ever visit The Waldorf Towers, or see me perform at a private event, you'll come equipped with information that I've never before wanted to release. The psychological secrets of how magicians influence their audiences will now be your secrets too. I look forward to meeting you.

WIN
the
CROWD

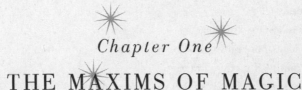

Chapter One

THE MAXIMS OF MAGIC

THE ART OF MAGIC has been around for thousands of years. Archaeologists have even found hieroglyphics depicting magicians performing sleight-of-hand tricks. Interestingly enough, those same tricks still baffle audiences today. We must be doing something right.

Think back to the first magic trick you ever saw. Maybe your cousin showed you a card trick at a family barbeque. Or you might've seen a magician pull a rabbit out of an empty basket. Or perhaps you saw a TV magician levitate a woman in midair. Can you remember your sense of wonder?

These tricks worked because the magicians followed a set of rules. Fortunately, anyone can learn and apply these rules to influence others. I use them not only onstage but offstage as well—with my family, friends, and business associates and in my community.

I call these rules the Maxims of Magic. Magicians follow them to convey confidence during their performances. Once you make the decision to do the same—to think like a magician—you will feel more confident yourself. People will sense your new positive attitude and respond by wanting to be around you and follow your lead.

Here, then, are the Maxims of Magic.

THE MAXIMS OF MAGIC

1. **Be Bold**

   Take risks—don't be shy about the actions you take or the words you speak.

2. **Expect Success**

   Start every personal encounter with the expectation that it will succeed.

3. **Don't State—Suggest**

   Use the power of suggestion instead of flat-out statements.

4. **Practice, Practice, Practice**

   Work hard privately so that you appear effortless in public.

5. **Be Prepared**

   Stay several steps ahead of your audience at all times.

Let's examine each of these rules in detail so that you can get started using them right away. Before you know it, you'll be casting your own spell over people whom you interact with on a daily basis.

MAXIM 1: BE BOLD

One of the things that separates beginning and experienced magicians is guilt. An important part of magic requires the performer to hide an object in his hand while keeping a perfectly straight face. This is tougher than it seems. It takes nerve. If you don't believe me, try it now. Clip a coin between your fingers so that no one can see it from the front. Now keep it there for the rest of the day, doing all of the things that you normally do. Eat meals, have meetings, speak to your family. Don't grip the coin so tightly that your fingers turn purple! Be natural. By the end of the day, you'll understand how hard it is to pretend that nothing's there.

Beginning magicians feel guilty that they are hiding something and unconsciously give off telltale signs. Audiences may not know exactly what the magician is hiding, or how he's hiding it. But they know he's hiding *something*. His guilt betrays him in the form of awkward gestures. The beginner may keep his arm frozen in place instead of letting it swing naturally. Or he might glance in the direction of the hidden object. This attitude spoils the illusion of magic, and audiences walk away with a big, fat question mark.

Experienced magicians are able to keep secrets from audiences without feeling guilty. We've learned how to act naturally, even when people are staring. I learned this early on when I was a child. I remember swiping a cookie from the cookie jar. I heard my parents approaching and had to make a quick decision. Should I fold my arms and hide the cookie so that my parents can't see it, or should I swing my arms naturally with the cookie in full view? I decided to hide it in full view. I took a deep breath, relaxed, and acted as if nothing unusual were occurring. It's counterintuitive to think that you could hide an object in plain sight. But it worked. Nobody expected me to be so bold. Cookie in hand, I walked past my parents, and they had no clue that I was anything but innocent. This simple deception hooked me on magic.

I'm not suggesting that you hide things from people on a regular basis. That's not the point. I'm suggesting that you learn to stretch your comfort zone. It's not easy to act natural when you're the center of attention. It takes guts. The first step at making this maxim part of your life is to stop being afraid of other people and what they think of you.

When you're bold, you will get results that you've never had before, because you're doing things that you've never done before.

When I read the previous sentence to a friend of mine, a successful businesswoman, she said, "That is *so* true!" She lives by the following aphorism: "Don't ask first; just apologize later." Instead of running a new idea by her boss, she just goes ahead and tries it out. According to her, too many "managers" are entrenched in their ways of doing things and are likely to say no to something new. She just plows ahead and does it on her own.

This is boldness in a nutshell. If your new plan doesn't work, you can always apologize later for running with it. If it does work, though, you're a hero. Are you willing to take risks like that? If you are, then you're on your way to understanding boldness.

Risky Behavior at the Bank

Magicians know that the rewards can be so much larger when you challenge yourself to take risks. Legendary Las Vegas magician Jimmy Grippo proved this one evening when he was in a bank. At 6:00 PM, Grippo noticed that the vault door was being closed for the night. Thinking fast, he removed a playing card from his pocket and scaled it into the vault as the door was being sealed shut for the evening. His aim was perfect, and the card slid inside, unnoticed by the guard.

Early the next morning, Grippo returned to the bank with a newspaper reporter. They met the bank manager, and Grippo convinced him to participate in a card trick. The magician introduced a deck of cards and subtly coerced the reporter to select a duplicate of the card in the vault—the nine of hearts. Grippo made the card vanish using sleight of hand, and then commanded the manager to open the vault. To Grippo's surprise, the manager refused. He explained that the vault was on a time lock, and *no one* could open the door until 8:00 AM that morning! The three of them waited several more minutes until eight o'clock rolled around, and the door clicked open. When the manager walked into the vault, the missing nine of hearts was sitting on the floor. Needless to say, the manager and reporter had witnessed a "miracle."

Let's back up and remember my friend's saying: "Don't ask first; just apologize later." If Grippo had been caught throwing the card into the vault the night before, he would have simply apologized to the guard and retrieved the card. If his aim had been off and the card hadn't landed perfectly in the vault, his attempt would've been foiled—but at least he'd have tried.

The message to take away from this story is that **you'll never know the outcome until you decide to take a risk.** Grippo received a feature story in the newspaper the next day. He could've received nothing. Since we magicians make our living based on reputation and word of mouth, that newspaper coverage was like pure gold. Worth the risk? I'd say so.

How Can You Become Bolder?

This is a great question, especially if you are normally a shy person who feels nervous in public. Fortunately, you don't have to make a leap to become bold. You can do it gradually. Throughout this book, you'll learn many new ways to increase your confidence, so that speaking up will become a piece of cake.

If you're supershy, start in a nonthreatening location, such as an elevator. The next time you are on the elevator with a stranger, break the silence and compliment her. That's right. Find something noteworthy about that person and say, "That's a nice [sweater/hat/watch] you're wearing. I like it." This simple *act* forces the person to *react*. You've taken a risk, and you've taken control of the situation. You've done something bold. Bravo! If the stranger ignores you, or thinks you're a creep, don't worry. You'll both be getting off the elevator soon enough. The pain of rejection will come and go so quickly that you'll never even notice it. If you're not in the habit of speaking to strangers, you'll be pleasantly surprised at how easily people will chat with you. If you're shy, challenge yourself to compliment five people daily. This is your first step toward conquering shyness.

Admittedly, this is a simple drill. Once you've gained confidence making "elevator friends," you can move on to the next level of boldness training: raising your hand.

A shy college student I met was terrified of being called on by the professor, so I advised her to be bold and do the very thing she was scared of— speak up voluntarily. Instead of waiting to be called on, she decided to take the initiative and raised her hand so she could contribute more aggressively in class—she made herself more visible by soliciting attention. She said that the hardest part of implementing this plan was the initial decision to overcome her fear of speaking up. Once she cleared that hurdle, though, it became more and more natural to participate in discussions. This seemingly simple decision helped raise her grades and earn her respect from her professor and her classmates.

If you hold back and wait for people to call on you, you could find yourself waiting forever. Instead of letting someone else determine how much or how little you are permitted to participate, speak up and make yourself more visible. If you have something funny to say, come out and say it. No need for apologies. If you have a strong opinion, it does no good bottled up inside your head.

As an entertainer, I've learned that people are fascinated by someone who is larger than life. They want to be around others who are more unique and interesting than themselves. If you hide your ideas, you are alienating yourself. Dare to speak up—you'll become more attractive to others, and your interactions with them will become more dynamic. You'll never know what it feels like until you start trying.

The Quarter Load

Your final drill—called the Quarter Load—will bring you to the cutting edge of boldness. If you're still afraid of other people, then you're not ready to try this. Go back to the first drill in this section and continue complimenting people in elevators. When you *are* ready to tackle the Quarter Load, you'll discover what it's like to take risks around other people, and the thrill that is attached to that risk.

At the beginning of this section, I taught you how to secretly clip a coin in your hand. Reread that description if you need to (see page 2) and hide a quarter in your hand right now. The next time you meet someone, I want you to do something crazy: drop your quarter into that person's pocket.

That's right. You're not picking pockets, you're *loading* pockets. Think of it as a game. The aim is to load the coin inside without getting caught. No need to feel guilty, since you're not stealing anything; you are actually making the person richer. At the end of the day, when he empties his pockets, he'll find an extra quarter inside. No harm done, right?

First I'll explain how to surreptitiously load someone's pockets, and then I'll tell you *why* you should practice this drill. (There's a method to my madness.) When you're with people, spot their pockets. You'll notice that some pockets tend to flare open more than others. These are the ones you'll practice on. (Don't bother with jeans pockets. They're too tight.)

You must contrive some way to come in close and touch the other person. Perhaps you'll hug an old friend who you haven't seen for a while. At the moment your hands go around him—slip!—drop the quarter into his outside jacket pocket.

If a man's shirt pocket is somewhat open, reach forward with your coin hand and tap the man's chest with the back of your fingers. Do this to emphasize a point that you are making verbally, such as, "John, you rascal! Where have you been hiding?" (Tap the chest when you say the word "rascal.") At the moment that you tap his chest—slip!—drop the quarter into his shirt pocket.

I have done this hundreds of times, purely as an exercise in boldness. Have I gotten caught? Sure, a few times. I was caught when I looked down too intently at the person's pocket. He'd stare at me funny and say, "You just *did* something." The key is to pretend that nothing unusual has happened. Once the coin has dropped inside, you will experience a small thrill—a personal victory. Don't spoil it by saying, "Hey—look in your pocket!" And also, please don't manhandle the person you're loading. The move requires only a nonthreatening, nonsexual pat on the body.

Now that you've learned the technique, I'll explain why you would ever want to engage in such unusual behavior. The reason you should practice the Quarter Load is to learn the thrill of going beyond your own comfort zone. This drill doesn't offend or harm anyone. It's purely a personal challenge that allows you to experience a small victory over another person.

When you've learned how to do something as silly as dropping coins into people's pockets, you've also internalized how to take other risks. People won't be as scary to you as they used to be. You'll feel more confident speaking up to them. You've learned how to navigate around people, so telling them your opinion should be less intimidating.

You'll begin to understand what I'm talking about once you've loaded your first coin. Go get a roll of quarters and start loading!

MAXIM 2: EXPECT SUCCESS

When I perform a trick, I know it's going to work. I've practiced it so many times that I feel confident showing it to others. What people don't realize, however, is that there may be several different endings to the same trick. As magicians, we plan multiple endings so we can bring the trick to a successful conclusion, no matter how many speed bumps we hit during the show. The audience only sees one of those endings, of course. If something goes wrong—such as a dropped prop or an unexpected comment by the audience—magicians smoothly shift to Plan B, with no one else the wiser. Since the audience doesn't know how the trick is *supposed* to end, they assume that they're seeing the only possible ending.

This concept of "knowing the endings" gives you a great deal of confidence. It enables you to expect a positive outcome no matter how your audience responds. My goal is to start every encounter—both onstage and offstage—with the expectation that it'll succeed. The way to do this is by thinking out in advance each of the possible desirable outcomes.

Sometimes, however, unexpected things happen when everyone is watching you. Should you panic, or apologize? Never! When you are in front of a group, never apologize when you notice that something has gone wrong. Other people probably don't even realize that anything is amiss. Remember: the only person who knows your intended outcome is you. Why draw undue attention to something that hasn't even crossed people's minds? As magician Al Baker wrote, "the wicked flee when none pursue."

When you are in front of a group and notice that something is amiss, you need to use "spontaneous resourcefulness." This term, coined by magician Bill Simon, suggests that you stay in the moment and fashion a solution on the fly. Since you have started the interaction expecting to succeed, your mind is geared to figuring out solutions. You recall similar situations that you've encountered in the past and apply your experience to solve the new challenge. When something has gone wrong in a presentation, interview, or other scenario, call forth all of your personal resources to discover a way out. You may have to resort to an ending that is not what you had originally planned. Sometimes the new outcome is surprisingly better than anything you could have anticipated.

I remember one performance I gave in Aspen, Colorado. I only had time to perform one trick. I chose to change a blue handkerchief into a red handkerchief. Although it appeared that only one handkerchief was in play, I in fact had a second one hidden in my hand. Unfortunately, some spectators on the side were able to see the hidden hanky. In magic lingo, I "flashed," showing the audience something that they weren't supposed to see. They called me on it, and I immediately rolled with the moment. I shifted my attitude so that it appeared the flash was intentional. I said, "Of course there are two handkerchiefs. How else could I do the trick? But since I have two, it makes it that much harder to make them both . . . vanish." At that, I made both of the hankies disappear. Everyone figured that this was the planned finale, but it wasn't what I had planned at all. And the crowd's reaction at my makeshift trick brought a bigger response than my intended trick.

How can you apply spontaneous resourcefulness? The key is to be well prepared (see Maxim 5, page 16, for more on this). If, for instance, you are going to a job interview, the worst possible scenario is having only one answer to a given question in your head. You can never fully control the direction of the interview, but you *can* prepare your core messages. Before you step in front of the interviewer, always plan out as many potential outcomes as you can. If you're "caught" with a tricky question, steer your answer toward one of your multiple core messages. Stand firm on your messages, and you will never appear to be flustered.

If you are in sales, you use spontaneous resourcefulness every time you sell something. Salespeople know that there are only four main answers: "Yes," "No," "Maybe," and some sort of smoke screen (e.g., "I need to speak with my [husband/wife/boss]"). Any one of these answers is a success, or could lead to a success. Even if the answer is no, that's a success because you know you don't have to waste any more time with that person. You don't despair, because you expected no as one of the outcomes.

I find that writing down the most likely outcomes in a pocket notebook helps me organize my thoughts, even at the last minute before a meeting. This simple preparation empowers you. It empowers you in two ways. First, you'll clarify to yourself the important points that you want to present. And second, if your mind happens to "go blank" during the meeting, you can refer to your notebook as a memory jog. I know it sounds simple, but you'll thank me the next time your mind goes blank and you're sitting there not knowing what to say. Glance down at your notes, check your core messages, and you'll be back in the game.

MAXIM 3: DON'T STATE—SUGGEST

We magicians don't *say* that we possess magical powers. Instead, we *suggest* that this is the case. I would insult your intelligence—you'd probably laugh at me—if I told you that I am a wizard with control over the mystical arts. However, I can lead you to believe this on your own through my attitude and carefully placed hints.

In general, people will believe their own opinions before believing yours. When you make a statement, the information in that statement is open to debate. After thinking about it, people might agree with you, but they could just as easily disagree. If, instead of stating, you make a suggestion, people will come to their own conclusions. This is more effective. Who will they believe more—you or themselves? Clearly, they will believe the conclusion they arrived at themselves, using their own experience and logic. Once people feel they've drawn their own conclusion, you've locked in your message without ever stating it outright.

You can make both verbal and nonverbal suggestions. We'll cover verbal suggestions in chapter 10, "Magic Words." In my own work as an entertainer, I've found that the nonspoken suggestions help set the stage even before I open my mouth. Novelists use this technique extensively. When an author wants you to think something about a character, he doesn't flatly write, for example, "John is sad." Instead, he may write "John's shoulders slumped forward, his eyes red from crying." Based on this description, the reader gets a better impression of the author's intentions. It's the old adage **Show, don't tell.**

When I perform for audiences, I think of myself as the author of the character I am portraying. I use any method necessary to enhance and develop that character for my audience. You can do the same, even if you're not in show business. Become the author of your own character. If you were a character in a book or movie, how would someone write about you? Are you wild and spontaneous? Or careful and detail-oriented? Do you wear your collar open or buttoned shut? Necktie or not? Shirt tucked or untucked? Does your look complement or contradict the image you want to present? Whatever you choose, aim to be consistent. Your look should always complement the personality you want to portray. In my show, I dress in a full tuxedo with tails. I wear an expensive watch, a shiny silk necktie, and a gold chain attached to my glasses. Offstage, I continue to dress in high-quality clothing that is consistent with my onstage look.

I recall meeting a young employee of a luxury hotel who violated this maxim. During working hours, he dressed in the same uniform worn by all of the front-desk attendants: jacket, necktie, and vest. Late one night, I happened to be in the lobby when I saw that employee leaving the hotel. At the end of his shift, he ducked into a back office and changed into his street clothes—a black T-shirt with the Ramones logo, torn jeans, and Converse high-tops. He walked through the hotel lobby and left through the front door. I couldn't believe my eyes. It was as if he were two entirely different people. Audiences need a more consistent message.

Remember, you are creating a character. Define it clearly and stick to it. Make yourself vivid. People often say to me, "You're all dressed up. Are you on your way to a show?" I answer, "No, I always dress this way." My character is that of a high-society entertainer. Yours will likely be very different. If you are a young professional, you may assume that you can dress as you please on your days off. You may believe that nobody is watching. If I've learned one thing in show business, it's that somebody is *always* watching. You'll bump into your boss, your colleague, or your best client when you least expect it. If they look down at your feet and see you wearing flip-flops when you should be wearing wingtips, it could affect whether they choose to continue doing business with you.

Decide what manner of person you wish to be taken for, and then dress the part. All of the time. At some stage in your life, this decision will force you to phase out your previous persona. Businesspeople are often faced with decisions like this when they've been promoted. Once they've moved into a corner office, should they continue socializing with their old cubicle buddies? In most cases, the answer is, unfortunately, no.

The suggestions you make with your new clothes and attitude will indeed cut you away from the old you. At first your new persona may feel awkward or put on, but you'll soon normalize at the next level. Later in this book (in chapter 3, "Create a Colorful Personality"), you'll learn how I did this, and how you can too.

MAXIM 4:
PRACTICE, PRACTICE, PRACTICE

One of the lessons that magicians are taught early on is to make the difficult look simple (or even invisible). The way to do this is through practice. What first seems impossible will eventually become reasonable after you dedicate yourself to the task. Remember, difficulty is a relative concept. What is difficult to you may be a breeze for somebody else. Through practice, you can master what you initially deem out of your reach.

Every morning since I was fourteen years old, I've practiced one of the most difficult secret moves in card magic: the Classic Pass. Done poorly, it can be seen from across the room. Done well, this technique is invisible. When an expert executes the Pass, the audience doesn't even realize that anything has happened. Before, during, and after the move, the deck of cards looks identical. There is no extraneous muscle tension in the fingers. There are no "tells." It is truly invisible.

I'll admit that it is somewhat frustrating to dedicate so many years to achieving a goal that nobody is supposed to see. In fact, nobody is supposed to even *sense* that something has happened. In addition to perfecting the hand motions, I've learned to relax my upper arms, my jaw, and even my eyes. When I first started learning the Pass, other magicians told me that my eyes fluttered at the moment that I executed the move. We recorded it on video, and I saw what they meant. (Video practice is better than mirror practice because you aren't executing the moves at the same moment you're examining them.) I broke myself of this poor habit through training.

Simply put, nobody wants to watch another person make something difficult *look* difficult. When we see people labor, it takes away from the experience and doesn't give us confidence in them. We like to see perfection, or something like perfection. We enjoy masterpieces, and masters doing their craft. Television shows us the instant replays of athletes like Michael Jordan making incredible shots. But they don't re-air the ones he missed. You expect to see others at the peak of their game, and guess what—they expect you to be at the top of your game too.

Salespeople are the best at making the difficult look simple. If you are involved in sales, you have intimate knowledge of this mind-set. You have to give presentations, overcome objections, think on your toes, and keep a positive attitude throughout. If the seams are showing—if customers can sense the flowchart as they're talking to you—the sale is lost. You have to take all of your theory and make it conversational.

How can you do that? The answer lies in carefully orchestrated practice. You probably cringe when you hear the word "practice." Perhaps you have painful memories of being forced to practice a sport or musical instrument when you were younger. You are not alone. Let's face it, there are few shortcuts to achieving excellence. Luckily, however, you can shave down your practice time by following some creative and fun strategies that will help you master your subject faster and more efficiently.

Dai Vernon, one of the greatest magicians who ever lived, professed that practice should be fun. You should derive great pleasure from practice, he said, or else give up the subject altogether. Make practice fun and you will be greatly rewarded. Do this by making a game of it. You'll learn my method below.

In the same way that bodybuilders isolate muscle groups when they train, you can isolate your skills. Here is how I practice a new magic trick so that it becomes second nature.

1. **Silence.** First, I perform the entire trick in silence. I do not speak as I go through the moves with props in hand. I focus only on the physical aspect of the performance.

2. **Motionless.** Second, I put all of the props away, and I speak the lines aloud that I will say during the trick. My hands hang at my sides, motionless. In this second stage, I focus only on the verbal expression of the performance.

3. **Darkness.** Third, I perform the entire package—props, body movement, spoken word—but I perform with my eyes closed. This forces me to rely on "muscle memory." I remember the relative position of where props are located and how far I need to reach for them.

4. **PP.** The final and in my mind most important stage is "PP," or "People Practice." I go out and perform in front of real people. No matter how well you've run through your motions and lines in a quiet room, the dynamics change dramatically when you present the same information to living, breathing people. In show business, entertainers usually find someplace they can "be bad" and break in new material—a no-name comedy club or other nonthreatening location, like a church or community center. You need a place to "be bad," where you can break in your sales pitch, your script, or your interview lines in front of live people.

Where can you find this mythic place? All around you, actually. The obvious first choice is to practice in front of your spouse or partner. However, I suggest you break in your material before people who don't know you so well. It puts you more on your guard. Some examples are your doorman, your neighbor, a store clerk, the mailman. These people are nonthreatening. If you flub a line, you've lost nothing. They won't hire you or fire you. They're painless. All you need is a live human. The feedback you receive from these people after running through your entire presentation will be immensely valuable—even more so than the first three steps, in many cases.

. . .

From my experience as a magician, I can assure you that this four-part process—Silence, Motionless, Darkness, PP—is fun to implement and will help you build confidence before you give your next presentation.

Practice Your "Outs"

As you practice, you'll make dozens of mistakes. Bravo! Better to make mistakes now than later. I've done my act so many times that I know everything that can go wrong. I've taken steps to prevent those things from happening during a live performance. Here are some examples of things that I pay attention to. What if a hidden prop falls out of my fist when people are watching? What if someone spills red wine on my clothing before the show begins? What if some audience members are drunk and they need to be removed from the room? What if someone dies during my show? Some of these scenarios may seem extreme, but each one has happened. And I'm ready for them, because I've practiced my "outs."

What are outs? Think of a fire drill. You go through all of the emergency procedures in advance so that they become second nature if, heaven forbid, you ever need to perform them for real.

As I mentioned in Maxim 2, magicians prepare hidden avenues in case something goes wrong. Outs are the way that we get out of precarious situations. I've spent hours practicing what I'll say when things go wrong. Professional entertainers have an obligation to present every audience with a graceful conclusion, no matter how flubbed things become.

As you practice your next presentation or talk, pay homage to Murphy's Law and intentionally handicap yourself. For instance, drop your notebook so that its pages scatter all over the floor. Then think of your out. What would you do if this happened for real? Wing your presentation from memory? Drop to your knees and try to collate everything while people wait? Have have an extra crib sheet printed on a note card in your pocket? Skip using a notebook altogether? Go through every possible solution that you can think of, and resolve them during your practice sessions. When it comes to showtime, you'll be more than ready because you've armed yourself with outs. This readiness translates into confidence, which is the aim of practicing in the first place.

MAXIM 5: BE PREPARED

There are always people in your life you need to impress—during job interviews, dates, business presentations, and so on. What price would you pay to *really* impress them? The best magicians will go to any extreme to win you over. Likewise, you should go to any extreme necessary if you want to stand out.

Advance preparation is one of a magician's key tools. Sometimes the preparation and handling take place in the first two minutes of a trick, when the audience thinks we are casually chatting. Other times, it is much more elaborate, with months—or even years—of planning. Magician Michael Weber says that you have to be so far ahead of the game that the audience shouldn't even know a game is being played. This means that you have to think ahead. *Really* think ahead, so that you set up the rules that others play by.

People will naturally assume that you haven't gone to that much trouble for them. But if, for instance, you are in the service business, taking extra steps will make an incredible impact.

Preparation boils down to knowing your audience. When someone hires me for an event, the first thing I do after hanging up the telephone is type the host's name into Google. I check his affiliations, political interests, previous addresses, and any media coverage. I then perform an image search on Google so I can see what he looks like. If you've never tried this, go to: http://images.google.com and type in the name of someone you know. Within instants, you'll be staring at a photograph of the person who you just spoke with on the phone. It's terrific.

(This only works for people who have posted their photos online or appeared in a news story.) As you can see, I arm myself with as much knowledge as I can about my new client. By the time we meet, I feel like I'm meeting an old friend. It's much easier to speak with someone you're already familiar with, since you don't have to build rapport from scratch.

This get-to-know-you technique is particularly valuable when you are applying for a job. Can you find out about the person interviewing you? How about working hard to really understand the company you're talking with? Can you talk to some people who have worked there? The key: do your homework. Go all out. Your preparation will empower you before you walk through the front door.

One of the reasons you may feel anxiety before a meeting or social encounter is because it will be held in a location that you've never been before. You may feel perfectly confident in your own office or home, but less so when you're the visiting team. As you'll learn in chapter 6, "How to Command a Room," part of a professional magician's preparation includes getting there early. You'll learn how to "own the stage" and boost your self-confidence.

Remember this: people expect that you'll do the *minimum* amount of preparation possible. Surprise them by doing a whole lot more. Be like Nostradamus and think ahead. Think things through to the nth degree before you walk into a meeting and you'll dazzle the other people there. They'll become excited to talk with you further because they won't be able to dismiss you. You'll know too much about them already, and, as you are aware, the most interesting topic of conversation for people is themselves.

THE VANISHING THOUSAND GRAINS OF SUGAR

Here is a magic trick that you can learn to do yourself. It incorporates all five Maxims of Magic, so you can see how magicians actually apply the rules you've learned. It's easy as pie, but mind-boggling to your audience. This is based on a trick by magician Brad Stine.

What the audience sees: Sitting in a restaurant, you tear open a sugar packet and pour all of the sugar into your fist. However, when you open your hand, all of the sugar has magically disappeared. It's really gone!

How you do it: This trick requires advance preparation. The sugar packet is actually empty to begin with. Nobody will know this but you.

Here's how you prepare the sugar packet. First, you must "steal" a sugar packet from the sugar bowl. ("Steal" is magic lingo. It means "Secretly remove something when nobody's watching.") You'll have to judge the right time to steal the packet. One way is to distract your companions. For example: "I wonder what those people at the next table are eating." The moment they look away, make your move and swipe the sugar packet. Sometimes you'll be lucky and there'll be a natural distraction (a waiter drops his tray, your companion's cell phone rings, etc.). Take advantage of these fortuitous moments and nobody will have a clue that you did anything sneaky.

Hide the packet under the table and use one of the pointy ends of your fork to puncture a small hole near one end. (Instead of a fork, you can use a pocket knife if you normally carry one.) Poke through only one side of the packet—not both. To avoid a mess, make sure that you shake all of the sugar down to one end of the packet before you puncture it. Tear the hole larger until it runs across the entire top short edge of the packet. The tear should be a little jagged-edged (not perfectly smooth)—later this will come in handy (see figure 1).

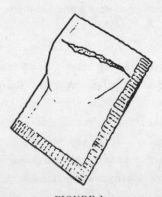

FIGURE 1.

Dump all of the sugar out of the packet except for a few grains. I suggest that you pour the sugar into a paper napkin that you've draped over your lap. After the napkin is full of sugar, crumple it into a ball and stick it in your pocket. This will ensure that nobody accidentally finds it after the trick is over.

Take your time with this preparation. Don't feel rushed. Nobody at the table will be aware that you plan to show them a trick later in the meal. If you've done this preparation early enough, there should be no heat on you. (Read the notes at the end of this trick's description if you find this step difficult.)

Find another moment to load the empty packet back into the sugar bowl. ("Load" is more magic lingo. It means "Secretly insert something when nobody's watching.") You're now ready to perform "The Vanishing Thousand Grains of Sugar."

To perform: Remove the prepared sugar packet from the sugar bowl. Rip off the top short edge, tearing along the same line that you used to empty the packet. You are only tearing through a single layer of paper, but the audience will think that you're tearing open the packet as usual. Since your secret tear was jagged, not smooth, this new tear helps destroy evidence of any preparation. Discard the little paper strip that you tore off.

Use your fingers to flare open the top of the packet. In a moment you are going to pretend to pour sugar into your fist. If the packet is too flat, this won't look realistic. Puff it open a little bit so that you can "pour" the sugar out.

Make a fist with your left hand. Hold the packet with your right hand and tip the opening toward your left fist. Continue to tilt the packet upside down and pretend to pour the sugar into your fist. This'll require a little acting on your part. Imagine what it would feel like to really pour sugar into your hand. Mimic this with your actions and facial expressions.

If you remembered to keep a few extra grains of sugar in the packet during the preparation, those grains will land on the top of your fist. They act as a convincer and lock in the idea that you've really poured sugar into your fist. Brush away those few grains and hold your (empty) fist high above the table. Discard the empty packet.

You're now ready to baffle your companions. Stare at your fist. Everyone will wonder what is going to happen. Suddenly open your hand. Your companions will be surprised that all of the sugar has disappeared!

The physical technique is not that difficult, so you can focus your attention on the presentation of this trick. As in all magic, what you *say* defines the experience for your audience. The same trick could be presented as a humorous gag or an unfathomable mystery, depending on how you cloak it. I like to present this trick as a mystery. Here's what I say during the performance.

"Do you think I could make one thousand objects disappear at the same time? It's never been attempted before. Let's give it a try. [Remove prepared packet from the bowl.] I'll pour the sugar into my fist. [Start pouring and count out loud.] That's six hundred grains . . . seven hundred grains . . . okay, one thousand grains of sugar. [Hold your fist over a dark napkin. If any grains drop, you'll see them on top of this napkin.] Are you ready? Watch how I squeeze my hand. Yes, it's starting to melt away! Now it's gone!"

COULD YOU pick out all five Maxims of Magic? Let's see how they were applied in this trick.

1. **Be Bold.** You took two risks before you even began. First, you stealthily removed the sugar packet when nobody was looking. Then, after you siphoned out all of the sugar, you waited for the proper time to slip the packet back into the bowl.

If you want to eliminate one level of boldness, go to the restroom earlier in the evening and swipe a sugar packet from another table on the way there. Prepare the packet in one of the restroom stalls, dumping the sugar down the toilet. When you return to your table, you must simply load the empty, prepared packet into the sugar bowl as you've already learned. That's bold enough a task on its own.

2. **Expect Success.** You began the trick with confidence, and others trusted that you knew what you were doing. They assumed that you wouldn't waste their time. When people have faith that you can complete a task, they give you temporary authority status. This converts into full authority status once you've proven that you could complete what you proposed.

3. **Don't State—Suggest.** You suggested that the sugar packet was full, without actually saying, "Ladies and gentlemen, this packet is full of sugar." That would've been a mistake. Because the sugar packet was in the bowl, you implied that the packet was full of the sweet stuff.

4. **Practice, Practice, Practice.** Although this trick is simple, simple doesn't mean easy. You should practice before attempting to perform it in front of a live audience. It may be helpful to *really* pour sugar into your hand once while practicing, so that you know what it's supposed to look like.

5. **Be Prepared.** You prepared this trick even before others knew that you planned to show them one. That's the spirit. Always strive to be several steps ahead of your audience and force them to play catch-up.

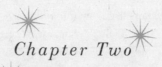

Chapter Two

CONVICTION: GIVE THEM
A MAGIC MOMENT

IT'S a THrILL TO see grown adults act like wide-eyed little children. It really is. I see it at every show. For the length of my performance, grown men and women *believe*. They believe in real magic. Their eyes sparkle as they gaze at the stage. They look as if they are lost in a fantasy that they wish would never end.

When we were children, we believed in many supernatural things—superheroes, the tooth fairy, and Santa Claus, to name a few. We also believed that magic was real. I remember when I realized this for the first time. I was entertaining at the Park Hyatt hotel in Tokyo, and a family had brought their four-year-old son with them. I made a red rubber ball disappear, showed my hands empty, and then pulled the ball from behind the boy's left ear. He said in Japanese, *"Mou ikkai yatte!"* ("Do that again!") Although the magician's code requires that you never repeat a trick, I did it again anyway. As soon as the ball disappeared a second time, the boy reached up to his left ear by himself and tried to pull the ball out. At that moment, I realized that he truly believed that magic is real. He believed that magic just *happens*. When balls disappear, he reasoned, they appear inside of people's ears.

Every time that you begin a new relationship, other people want to believe that you are the real deal. When I walk onstage, the audience wants to believe that I possess real magical abilities. Similarly, when you get hired for a new job, your employer wants to believe that you can deliver what you promised during the interview process. When you sell something, your new customer wants to believe that working with you and your company is the correct choice. It's your job to fulfill that belief.

To do this, magicians use a technique known as the Magic Moment. It's based on Maxim 3: Don't State—Suggest. We create the Magic Moment through a simple gesture, like waving a magic wand or wiggling our fingers. After a dramatic pause, we show the results of that gesture. But let's be honest here. Does the wand wave actually *do* anything? Do the wiggling fingers really make magic happen? In the context of the performance, they certainly do. But in reality, such gestures are theatrical devices that magicians use to build conviction.

When I'm performing, my onstage persona believes that I have real magic powers. The silent script that I recite to myself while performing convinces me that I am for real. When I wiggle my fingers, I can actually *feel* magical energy radiating from my fingertips.

But I'm not living in a fantasy world. Onstage, I am an actor playing the part of a magician. I know that if I want people to believe in me, I must believe in myself first.

Likewise, if you want people to believe in you, then believe in yourself first.

Conviction is what sells audiences on you. Every person you meet is part of an audience that is observing you, evaluating you, and hoping to believe in you. If you can convince them that you are able to deliver what they expect, then you will have gained a believer.

The good news is that you need not go out and buy a magic wand or practice wiggling your fingers in a quirky kind of way.

Instead, decide right now that you will simply believe in yourself. You are a unique person, and nobody is better at being you than you are; no one can do what you do the way you do it. Believe that you are capable. Believe that you are lovable. Believe that you are an expert, a pro, a smooth talker, and a slam-dunk presenter. Believe that you are the best. If you like, stick a little reminder over your bathroom mirror that reads, "I'm the best and deserve nothing but the best!"

If you think this is just rah-rah positive thinking, you're missing the point. In my experience, the Magic Moments—when I demonstrate conviction in my abilities—are what make people buy into me. Conviction is contagious.

Let's look at how you can magically make others believe in you.

THINK THAT YOUR WORK IS IMPORTANT

One of my favorite stories is about three bricklayers and their job attitudes. Someone asked the three laborers, "What are you doing?" The first bricklayer replied, "Laying brick." The second replied, "Making ten dollars an hour." But the third said, "Me? I'm building the world's greatest cathedral."

I love the attitude of that third bricklayer. He knows that his work is important, despite what others may think of such a "lowly" occupation. To be honest, I know that "magician" is not viewed as a highly prestigious occupation. Once when I listed my occupation as magician on a passport application, the government clerk laughed when he read the page. He pointed at my ski cap and snickered, "Are you going to pull a rabbit out of your hat?" When I tell people at parties that I am a magician, they occasionally ask, "So what's your *real* job?" They can't imagine that magic is somebody's full-time career.

Of course, I believe differently. To a professional conjuror, "magician" is the most important occupation in the world. Who else but a magician can provide the gift of laughter and wonder? Who else can let people live in fantasy for a short time before returning to their ordinary lives? We professional magicians have convinced ourselves that magic is a serious and worthy job.

Whatever field you have chosen, your work is important. Think this to yourself every day: "I am important. I do a first-rate job. I perform my work with dignity."

Don't fall into the trap of saying, "I'm just a housewife" or "I'm just a clerk." You are not "just" anything. Forget any stereotypes people may have about you or your occupation. When you believe in yourself, your actions become more definite. People observe your actions, and they see that you take yourself and your work very seriously.

We all learn by imitation. Of course, we know this about children, but it holds true for adults too. Think of how you and your best friend share similar slang or mannerisms. Your boss, your clients, and your children learn how to respect your work by observing how you respect it yourself. When you raise the bar of expectation, people will rise to the new level that you have set. Many people who come to my magic shows first believe that magic is silly, or just for kids. However, once audiences see me taking my magic seriously, they do the same. Audiences no longer heckle me, because they recognize that I've created an environment that's based on mutual respect, not a free-for-all.

No matter where you are in your career, treat your work with dignity. Even the bricklayer could see greatness in his labor. Give yourself a mental promotion and see yourself as a leader that others look to for guidance.

THINK OF YOURSELF AS A CELEBRITY

Take a moment and think about someone you consider an important person. It could be anyone—your supervisor, your spouse, a celebrity, a politician, anybody at all. Perhaps you consider this person important because of his power or her celebrity. It could be someone you know, or it could be someone you've admired from afar. Now imagine that *you* are just as important. Picture yourself being "an important person." It gives you a reason to puff out your chest, knowing that others feel that way about you. This is not to suggest you should become self-important. Rather, consider yourself as being the object of others' admiration.

When I walk out onstage, I assume that everyone already adores me. I don't try to win them over. I simply welcome them into my "circle of fun" (a marvelous phrase coined by magician Don Alan). If you assume that people are your adversaries, you have to work doubly hard. Assume that others have mentally selected *you* as their important person. Assume that the room lights up when you enter it. Assume that everyone's eyes are on you, because you are a celebrity.

Me? A celebrity? That's right. Imagine you're a celebrity. The word "celebrity" doesn't mean someone who is constantly involved in tabloid scandals. It refers to the fact that we celebrate something about these people. We celebrate their

ability—athletic, artistic, performing, moneymaking;
beauty—models, actresses, actors; and
power political, business.

In many ways, we celebrate these people because they have achieved something that we ourselves wish we had. I've met and entertained many celebrities over the years and have come to realize that we all have cause to celebrate similar attributes in ourselves. Nobody is better than you just because they are more well known. The ability, beauty, and power we find on the front page of gossip magazines are deep within us all. We celebrate those who have exhibited these attributes most prominently. But this doesn't mean you don't measure up. It simply means you may not be demonstrating your full potential.

Each time you speak, think to yourself, "Is this how an important person would say this?" When you dress to go out, think, "Would an important person dress this way?" When you get upset, think, "Would a successful person argue over this?" Mentally frame all of your behavior through this filter: "Would an important person . . ." Or, "Would my boss . . ." You will be surprised to find that your behavior will automatically adjust to your ideal level. Others will recognize the respect you have for yourself and will offer you theirs in return.

MOVE WITH A DEFINITIVE PURPOSE

When you move, move with precision and accuracy. You will assure the audience that you know exactly what you are doing. Remember, you are being observed by audiences all the time. Fumble or stumble, and you lose credibility.

Think of the actions you perform regularly. Do you strike like an expert? Or do you hesitate before moving? I remember the superintendent in my first apartment building in New York. He was awkward with his hands. While a professional repairman appears confident by moving with precision and accuracy, my apartment's superintendent would tap his fingers and roam his hands about as he attempted to figure out how to fix a simple leak. Needless to say, he was fired from the building. Lack of precision invites doubt in one's abilities.

On the other extreme, I met a basketball coach at the U.S. Military Academy at West Point who was able to sink ten out of ten jump shots. Every time. He moved like a machine. His form during each shot was the mirror image of that during every other shot. He was perfect. And naturally, he was a highly respected coach to the army team.

Actors call such precision "hitting your mark." Night after night, actors are expected to arrive at precisely the same location onstage to deliver their lines. If an actor is two inches off his mark (or spot onstage), the preset lights won't shine on him fully. He could be standing in shadow if he doesn't move the right way every time.

People are always watching you, whether you are aware of it or not. You want to instill confidence in them to make yourself worthy of their respect. When I lived in Japan, a tea ceremony master taught me a rule that clarified this point. The rule is: Think each action through before performing it. It's simple. *Think before you move.* Let's see how this works in the tea ceremony, and then how you can apply this rule.

The Japanese tea ceremony (*Chaji*) is a lesson in perfection. Guests enter the tearoom through a small door only thirty-six inches high. They are required to crouch down onto the tatami mats and slide themselves in with head bowed. This serves the dual purpose of creating equality between the guests and forcing them to offer respect to the tearoom. The last person who enters latches the door. After a delicate meal of miso soup, vegetables, fish, and rice, the master prepares tea for each guest. This procedure takes years to perfect. Just as some students join a sports team or drama group in high school, many Japanese students join the tea ceremony club. From an early age, they learn each choreographed movement, from the lifting of a pair of chopsticks to the folding of a handkerchief. Every action is performed the same way, every time. Students learn the proper way to pick items up, hold them, and set them down. The actions are never rushed but are performed with diligence and care. The tea master has internalized each of these movements until she can perform them without faltering. Through thousands of repetitions, the master knows each step and what comes next. And then she does it so it looks natural.

Remember this rule: Think before you move. I applied this to my magic, and you can apply the same rule to your life. Before you even lift a pinky, think of how you will start, execute, and finish the action. All of your thinking should take place before you begin.

This is how the tea ceremony master taught the rule to me. Try it with me now.

Trial 1

With your right hand, pick up a pen that is on the right side of your desk. Now reach across your body to your left side and place the pen down on your desk somewhere off to the left. It doesn't matter where. Just place it somewhere on the left side of your desk and leave it there.

Trial 2

Repeat the action as in Trial 1, but this time, decide *exactly* where you will place the pen on the left side of your desk *before you begin*. Remember: don't make a move until you've already decided where the final destination will be. Now pick up the pen and move it directly to that spot.

Did you feel the difference? In Trial 1, you had to make a decision as your hand was in transit. "Where should I put the pen down? Over here, or perhaps over there?" Sure, it's a quick decision, but it required thought nonetheless. In Trial 2, you knew exactly where the start and finish points were, and you moved more efficiently.

Strive to make all of your actions decisive, as you did in Trial 2. Think before you move. Whether you're handing a pen to a colleague for his signature, or flipping pages in a sales brochure for a client, make your actions precise. Mentally "feel" your body cutting through the air. Visualize the action, and then carry it out.

BLUFF WITH CONVICTION

I have a magician friend who is great at speaking with conviction. Even when he doesn't know the answer to something, he'll say, "I'm absolutely certain that I don't know the answer to that question." People who hear him say this feel that they are in good hands. They believe they are with someone who is *absolutely certain*. Sure, he's absolutely certain that he doesn't know the answer (!), but he sounds so decisive because of his strong use of language.

As often as possible, make an effort to sound like you know what you're talking about. This may sometimes require that you bluff. I don't advocate lying, because it's not in my nature. But I do suggest that you take risks to advance others' belief in you.

Once, my teacher Johnny Ace Palmer used sheer bluff to enhance his performance of a classic magic trick—the penetration of a finger ring through a shoelace. (In magic lingo, this trick is called "Ring and String.") In the traditional method, the magician holds both the ring and the lace, and the entire trick occurs in the magician's hands. An audience member once challenged Johnny by threading the ring onto the center of the lace himself, wrapping the ends of the string around his fist several times to completely trap the ring. There clearly was no way to make the ring penetrate the lace under such stringent conditions. The man asked, "Can you make it come off now?" Without flinching, Johnny confidently replied, "Sure." Even though it was truly impossible to remove the ring using traditional magic techniques, he shrugged his shoulders as if saying, "What a breeze." The man's face melted as he fell for the bluff. He was amazed that Johnny could do what he claimed and handed everything back without demanding proof.

If you must bluff, keep a firm gaze and speak slowly and confidently. Don't betray your lack of knowledge or ability by saying anything out of place. You may feel giddy in your stomach. It's natural to feel that way because you're taking a risk, and *you're experiencing it in real time*. People are watching you. Gamblers feel the same way when they try to convince their opponents that they hold better cards than they really do.

Whatever you do, don't show your insecurity outwardly. The best bluffs occur when you stay calm and assertive.

Remember this strategy the next time you quote a price for any service or product you are selling. Always ask for a higher price than you think you deserve. The other person may indeed say yes! But they will only agree to this price when you act with conviction and confidence. If you appear on the outside the way that you feel on the inside, it is highly unlikely that the deal will take place at your asking price. In order to receive the higher fee, you must make the buyer feel certain that you always get paid that much for similar jobs. Act as if the higher fee is par for the course. Assuming you can deliver what you are selling, this new rate will become your standard fee.

Once you've established your higher fees, you will have more confidence in booking jobs with future clients.

GIVE IT TIME

It would be wonderful if you could walk onstage and have everyone love you instantly. But even the most successful entertainers and presenters need to build up their credibility over a short period of time. Comedians know that they need to accumulate several laughs before they have the au-

dience in the palm of their hand. The first time that you act with conviction, people may not even notice. However, through consistency and rep-
etition you'll prove to others that you are indeed the real deal.

In my own shows, I've noticed that it takes three tricks before the
audience surrenders their skepticism. During the first trick they are on
their guard. During the second trick they start to come around. After the
third trick they think, "Okay, this guy is good." At that moment, they hand
over the reins and let me take them for a ride.

In your life, it's not likely that you've got an audience seated in front of
you. You're on the move, at meetings, luncheons, and golf weekends. For
that reason, it's more difficult for you to cultivate respect from your peers.
You may feel frustrated that others don't take to you right away. You see
them once, they are underwhelmed by you, and they move on. What can
you do about this?

Here is a suggestion. Don't give up so soon. Rejection is nothing to
fear. Each time you are rejected by someone, you're one step closer to
building a relationship with that person. Remember, it takes me three
tricks—about a quarter of my show—to get people on my side. If I were to
stop after only the first or second trick, I'd be frustrated too. I'd lament,
"Why didn't I capture that audience? Those were killer tricks! What did I
do wrong?" It took years of performing to discover that building credibility takes time. It's foolish to think that any one trick, joke, or passage can
win over an audience instantaneously. You need to prove yourself trustworthy. You need to surpass the mental threshold that your audience has
internalized. After my third trick, I know they've bought into me. If I quit
before that third trick, I may have mildly amused them, but they won't be
talking about me tomorrow around the water cooler.

Here's a suggestion for getting others to trust you. Count the number
of interactions that you have with each person. Keep a notebook and
record how many times you meet in person, how many times you speak on
the phone, and how many times you exchange e-mails. If you find that
your communication with a particular person isn't going as you had
planned, give it a little time. You may only have performed your first or
second trick. Don't give up. It's amazing to me how many people give up

after sending out one or two sales letters. Or they call someone one or two times. Even after the second call, you're still an unknown quantity. Most people need three or more impressions of an advertisement before they'll remember that they've seen it.

The magic will occur during your third and fourth call. Or your third and fourth meeting. If you're making a request to someone, ask at least three times. Remember, you probably haven't registered on their mental radar until after your third request.

This new attitude will help make rejection much easier. Some of my audience members are still skeptics after my first trick. They may think that magic is hokey—that it's for children, not adults. But their resistance doesn't rattle me. I just put a mental check mark next to the number one. I think, "Two more tricks to go." I push forward with the second trick. I think to myself, "They're still not responding. Hang in there." I weather the second phase of resistance with the knowledge that I've almost reached their threshold. I find a transformation in people's faces at the end of the third trick. They have no more reason to resist my advances once I've proven myself worthy of their attention.

Instead of being something to fear, rejection is something you can embrace. Each time you face rejection from someone, mark it off in your notebook. You're one step closer to building a relationship with that person. Such a simple shift in your thinking makes an enormous change in the way that you deal with rejection.

DON'T BELIEVE YOUR OWN PRESS

The conviction-building techniques described in this chapter will help you believe in yourself, if you apply them. As a result, you will seem more trustworthy to others. They will begin to believe in you more often. However, there is an easy trap that you can fall into as well: believing yourself too much.

When you start to believe your own press, you allow control to shift into the hands of others. Broadway actors are often advised not to read their own reviews. Such information would affect their artistic vision. In its extreme, the unwavering belief in others' opinions of you and your work is akin to giving your life or your spirit away. While it is worthwhile to listen to informed outside opinions, it is also worthwhile to install a mental valve so you can turn them off.

All magicians have internalized a reality/fantasy valve. The valve has two marked settings: Reality and Fantasy. If the valve were always switched to Fantasy, magicians would be living in a dream world. In this scenario, when a lit cigarette appears at his previously empty fingertips, the magician would truly believe that he plucked it from thin air. And when a dollar bill transforms into a hundred-dollar bill, the magician would be convinced that he can multiply money all day long. Such behavior would be considered delusional, and the target of psychiatric help.

That's where the mental valve becomes important. When we devise our tricks, magicians flip the valve to Reality. We are forced to work in the material world, which is based in natural and unbreakable laws. Magicians simply apply those laws in unique ways to offer you the experience of magic. Like actors, we flip the valve back to Fantasy when we are on-stage. That's when we let the fantasy fly, and our characters appear to enjoy the rush of commanding nature.

How can you install such a mental valve? It's simple. When someone honors you in front of your peers, step back and be objective. Are you suddenly *better* than them? Whenever someone calls you "the best," ask yourself whether you *really* are the best at what you do. Of course not. You can always improve. It's wonderful to be praised, but use that praise to push yourself forward, not rest on your laurels. Flip your valve to Reality so you don't get enveloped in the warm glow of mediocrity.

People will respect you even more when they see that you aren't lost in the fantasy of your reputation. One day after a show I performed in Hawaii, I met a man who had been in the audience the night before. We spoke for about ten minutes, and I repeatedly deflected his insistence that I was the greatest magician in the world. Instead, I asked him questions about himself and his family. At the end of the conversation, he said, "I had no idea that you would be so approachable." His parting line clarified to me that people will respect you more when you aren't completely wrapped up in the mythological you. They want to see your genuine side. Show them that you're a real person. Instead of talking about how wonderful you and your work are, shift the focus to *them* and people will remember their experience with you as a positive one.

The more successful you become, the more public you become. And therefore, more people will recognize and approach you. Will they praise you? Sure. Get used to it. It's marvelous when you have an ability that affects people so strongly that they want to tell you about it. Consider yourself a celebrity, just not an arrogant one. Make it your practice to always turn the tables on people who rave about you.

Just remember to keep your valve switched to Reality. Don't believe their gushing for one second. If you do, you'll be on the path to self-destruction, and you'll actually lower your own status in those people's eyes. Strive to be genuine, not unreachable. You'll make a much more positive impression when people feel that they've met a person they can talk to. Think of any well-known people you've met. Who stands out more: the celebrities who treated you like another fan, or those who treated you like an individual?

SHIFTING THE COMPLIMENT

Magicians receive compliments all the time. After a well-executed trick, audiences respond immediately. They're excited, and they express their excitement through praise. I've learned how to handle such constant complimenting through a simple strategy that helps make the person giving the compliment feel even better about their exchange with you.

Now you can learn this strategy too. When someone compliments you:

1. **Say thank you.** It's amazing how many people feel uncomfortable accepting praise! Get used to saying thank you. That's what the compliment-giver wants to hear. If you're silent after receiving praise, you appear smug. "Thanks" is a little too flippy and sounds like you

haven't fully acknowledged the compliment. Say the two words, "Thank you," with confidence and maintain eye contact.

2. **Ask a personal question back.** Shift the focus of the exchange back to the compliment-giver. Ask a personal question to involve him or her. Tie your question to the subject of the person's compliment, so it'll flow more naturally.

PERSON: "You look great in that outfit."

YOU: "Thank you. You look like you know something about fine clothes yourself. Can you recommend a good tailor?"

PERSON: "That was a wonderful presentation."

YOU: "Thank you. I was a little nervous. Do you ever get nervous when you talk in front of people?"

PERSON: "You're the best magician I've ever seen."

YOU: "Thank you. Have you ever been to Las Vegas? You'd love the shows out there."

Do you see how each of these conversations shifts the focus back to the other person? It's simple, but believe me, it's easy to forget to do this. When someone compliments me, I'm tempted to say, "Thanks. Tell me more about how great I am." You may have developed a similar pattern of milking a compliment. Use this new strategy and break your old habit. People want to be recognized, even when they are recognizing you.

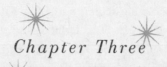

Chapter Three

CREATE A COLORFUL PERSONALITY

If they like you, they'll like what you do.
Nate Leipzig, magician and vaudeville star in the 1920s

STREET MAGICIANS USE BRIGHTLY colored props to catch the eyes of people who are on their way to someplace else. They use colors such as hot pink and fluorescent orange, both of which contrast sharply with most gray city streets and can be seen from yards away. That's the immediate goal: to capture people's attention from a distance and tickle their curiosity. Brightly colored scarves, cards, and hats cause people to act impulsively. Such flashes of color force them to think, "I wonder what's going on over there." And then they walk over.

Let's test what you're wearing now. Walk over to a mirror and squint your eyes. Your reflection will appear blurred. Despite the hazy image, any vivid colors you're wearing will pop to the forefront. It's just like that in real life. Whether you're on the street or in a room with other people, dozens of distractions compete for their attention. You're just a blur in the room until people consciously decide to focus on you. If you're wearing a muted color such as beige, you'll have a hard time standing out.

Ask yourself: "Is my personality beige?" If it is, you need to consider ways to become more colorful yourself.

A COLORFUL PERSONALITY

It's much easier to adorn your body in colorful clothes than it is to become colorful yourself. Shopping for clothing requires no more than a credit card. A colorful personality requires that you change your lifestyle.

Street magicians capture audience attention with colorful props, but they *maintain* that attention with a colorful personality. They act flamboyantly, and a little brash. They may even insult the audience.

My favorite street magician, Gazzo Macee, makes numerous lewd jokes and insinuating comments throughout his act. Seems risky, but it's psychologically sound. Audiences can't ignore someone who's larger than life. Whether or not they approve of your views, they're compelled to pay attention, just to hear what you'll say next. It's like driving by a roadside accident: even though people want to avert their gaze, they can't help but look.

Are you willing to offend other people? That's what'll happen when you have strong ideas. Entertainers and artists take this gamble every time they express themselves in their work. To paraphrase Abraham Lincoln, "You can't impress all of the people all of the time." If you're not offending some members of your audience, then you're probably too middle-of-the-road. The idea is to impress more people than you offend. Despite his brashness, Gazzo consistently pulled the largest crowds at Canada's annual busker's convention for many years. Several times he was crowned the winner of the entire convention, based on having earned the most amount of money from audiences. Obviously, he must have done something right. Audiences were amused by his up-front personality and paid handsomely to see it.

This doesn't give you license to curse people out in the name of notoriety. It does mean, though, that you should consider ways to really stand for something—an ideal, or a style. World-famous magicians Siegfried and Roy said, "Greatness is he who reminds you of no other."

Become larger than yourself by emphasizing the things you're great at and deemphasizing the things you're not. Dare yourself to stand out. Dare to do things that others aren't doing. When you dare to be bold, you also dare to be great.

My friend Jay was hired as the fashion director of a major fashion design firm. Nobody knew him, so he had to figure out a way to stand out. He found that he became more respected by his new peers when he exaggerated his style. Instead of toning down his normal street-cool look, he emphasized it and wore misstitched jeans, jackets with sagging linings, and wild color combinations. His look gave him confidence to act within his new career. He spoke out like he never had before, giving his clients firm guidance and mandates instead of wishy-washy opinions and timid advice. He put his career on the line every time he presented to clients. And they loved it. He stood out like no one they had seen before. As a result, his salary hasn't doubled or tripled—it's *quintupled* in a single year!

Will you upset people by speaking your mind and not holding back? Absolutely. However, strong conviction and belief in your own abilities will give you the confidence you need to get more people to join you than reject you.

Comedian Bill Cosby said, "I don't know the key to success, but the key to failure is trying to please everybody."

Don't become upset when people try to knock you down or voice their disdain. It's natural that you can't please everybody. Some people will respond negatively because they are negative people. They feel empowered by putting others down. Let their disdain empower you. The fact that people disagree with you at all signifies that you're making yourself more visible. For that you should be proud of yourself. There's no need to hide.

STICK YOUR NECK OUT

This is not an unfounded opinion. In my own career, I've offended some people with my moniker: The Millionaires' Magician. They felt that this title was too elitist. When I first called myself The Millionaires' Magician, many people around me told me that I was making a big mistake. My manager, my publicist, and even my wife thought that it was a foolish maneuver to make such a bold statement.

However, ever since I started using this title, my business has taken off. It's helped me win over more people than I've offended.

A magazine wrote a feature story about my show, calling me "The Millionaires' Magician." At first, I felt funny calling myself that. Sure, most of my clients were millionaires. And I figured that it was okay if the media called me this, since they were an unbiased third party. But wouldn't it be presumptuous or off-putting for me to use that title myself?

I hesitated for about two weeks. During that time, I consulted with branding expert Mark Levy, who recommended that I read a book by Al Reis entitled *Focus*. Reis advises that you pare away everything that is superfluous to your target market until you are focused entirely on one area of expertise. Companies that offer too many products or services can be beaten by a company that specializes in only one. I extrapolated this idea and made the decision that would change my career.

At Mark Levy's urging, I started to publicly call myself The Millionaires' Magician. I raised my rates and focused solely on performing for the social elite. I changed my Web site to reflect this new image and printed up expensive business cards with gold-embossed ink. The cards read: THE MILLIONAIRES' MAGICIAN, ENTERTAINMENT FOR EXCLUSIVE EVENTS. I bought some expensive hand-tailored Italian suits from Domenica Vacca, my favorite tailor in New York, and a gorgeous Franck Muller chronograph watch. More important than all of the physical trappings, though, I changed my outlook on how to do business.

No longer would I take any job that came my way. I decided to turn down requests that were not right for my new business direction. I simply said no to people who called. It is difficult to reject someone who wants to offer you money or a contract. But I knew that I needed to set a precedent. Like Reis wrote in *Focus*, when you define your abilities, you distinguish yourself from others in your field. I did not want to be seen as someone who could be bargained down. I decided that I would be the high apple on the tree that others need to reach for.

Luckily, this persistence paid off. And luckily, you can do the same. It is as simple as making a decision. Michelangelo said that each slab of marble contained a statue inside. All he needed to do was carve away the excess until the statue was exposed. You can do this in your life and in your career. Decide exactly how you want to be seen by others. Then carve away the parts of your life that no longer fit into your new image of yourself.

Will you feel uncomfortable at first? Sure. It's like trying on a new pair of shoes that need breaking in.

As media and corporate bookers began to recognize my new title, things started to come together. Since it is a colorful phrase, The Millionaires' Magician stuck in people's minds. Reporters latched onto it and ran stories about me in newspapers and on television.

All of this is because of one decision I made to define myself in colorful language.

UNCOVER YOUR HIDDEN TRAITS

You'll be delighted to know that you don't need to create a character at all. Your colorful character lives inside you right now. Your job is simply to let it out.

Take an honest look at yourself. Uncover the traits you already have. Developing a character is a process of self-discovery. It requires that you examine your motivations, your physical traits, and your values. The worst thing you can do is attempt to copy someone else. Think of the traits that make you distinctly you.

TRUE TALES
FROM THE MILLIONAIRES' MAGICIAN

For your entertainment, I've peppered this book with several anecdotes of memorable magic performances. Here is the first one.
You'll find more at the end of later chapters. I hope you enjoy reading
them and seeing how I've used the techniques of a showman to capture and command people's interest.

Anecdote 1
THE FLYING EARRING

Before serving dessert at a dinner party in New York, my host asked
that I do a little something for the guests. I declined politely, but
when people hear that there's a magician at the table, they expect to
see a trick.

I turned to the woman seated next to me and asked for one of her
earrings. She was hesitant to remove one of her diamond studs for a
magic trick. She thought I might damage it. But when our host nod-
ded his approval, she handed it to me.

"The Flying Earring Trick!" I announced, holding up my left
hand to silence the guests. The glittering diamond earring rested in
my left hand, which I slowly closed into a fist. I explained that I
would make the earring fly from one hand into the other, invisibly.
All of the guests looked at me with skepticism as I opened my left
hand: empty. They craned their necks in closer. I then opened my
right fist: also empty. The lady's face turned pale.

"If the earring didn't fly into my other hand, it could only have
gone one other place." I pointed to her ear, and her hand darted upward. She screamed in shock as she discovered that her earring had
reappeared *pierced* in her ear.

It was several minutes before everyone calmed down enough so
that dessert could be served.

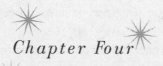

Chapter Four

BUILDING CONFIDENCE
BEFORE THE CURTAIN RISES

WaITInG In THE WInGS to speak can be nerve-wracking. The anticipation kills many speakers before they even begin.

Magicians use preparation and relaxation techniques similar to those used by other theatrical performers. This chapter teaches you how to eliminate stage fright and increase your confidence. First, let's work on your attitude.

ARE YOU MASTER OR SLAVE?

An unspoken power struggle exists in every personal interaction. One person controls the progress of the interaction, while the other follows his lead. It's like a master leading his slaves. Following is usually easier, since it requires less thought and initiative. However, those who lead earn more respect and admiration. I urge you to be the master, and not the slave. Have more self-confidence and expect that others will respect and listen to *you*. Your expectation will send off silent signals, telling others that they won't be able to walk all over you. Unfortunately, I had to learn this the hard way, by being walked on many times.

Early in my career I performed at dozens of bar mitzvah receptions. I cringe when I think about them now. My job was to stroll among the un-chaperoned twelve- and thirteen-year-olds and entertain them with close-up magic. Don't get me wrong. I love close-up magic, and I loved the fact that I was being paid to perform. What didn't sit well with me, however, was the unchaperoned twelve- and thirteen-year-olds part.

At these events, the youngsters would sometimes work in teams to fluster me and try to figure out my secrets. I remember one party where a group of boys huddled together, like a football team, and plotted out a strategy to upset the next trick. I could just imagine what they were saying. It must have been something like, "I'll watch his right hand, you watch his left hand. Ready . . . break!" Not knowing that I was walking into a trap, I started performing. Just when it was time to perform the secret move that would make the trick work, one kid dropped to his knees and watched from below, a second kid reached into my coat pocket, and a third kid grabbed my sleeve to see if anything was stuffed inside. I remember feeling humiliated. Not only did they ruin my trick, they also reduced me to a weaker social position. Clearly, they were the masters of the situation. I was the slave.

I chalked that up to experience and vowed never to let anything similar happen again.

THINK LIKE A MAGICIAN

Historically, magicians were powerful individuals in society. Instead of being taunted by groups of teenagers, they were respected by all. The village elders listened to shamans—the world's first magicians—and based important decisions on their advice. While few modern-day magicians have the ears of political leaders, we still symbolize control over our immediate environment. In a deck of fortune-telling tarot cards, one of the most powerful cards depicts a magician. On that card, a man points up to the heavens with one hand, while using a magic wand to point to the earth with the other. The magician is the conduit through which power flows from the natural to the supernatural world.

That's pretty heavy stuff. But it should help you recognize that thinking like a magician will help boost your self-confidence.

When I walk in front of new people, I assume that they already love me. I speak to them as if we are equals. Promise that you'll do the same. Never assume that someone is better than you. Even when you meet a CEO, a personal hero, or your dream client, treat him as a personal equal. Don't appear arrogant, be proud. Start every personal interaction from a position of strength, not weakness. I first learned how to do this when I read a classic book of magic, *New Era Card Tricks*.

More than one hundred years ago, in 1897, the book's author, August Roterberg, wrote: "The performer's manner should be suave, but not over polite, a mistake made by most beginners. Over politeness tends to reduce the performer to a level below that of the spectators." His point? If you retain a certain confidence, people will respect you more.

This was reinforced to me when I presented my magic show at the Ritz-Carlton in San Francisco. The Ritz-Carlton chain is renowned for its exceptional service. When employees join the company, part of their extensive training includes learning the corporate motto: "We are ladies and gentlemen, serving ladies and gentlemen."

Sure, the word "serving" appears in the motto, but it doesn't mean that the staff is subservient. They treat guests with respect, while expecting the same level of respect in return.

Each employee is issued a small card that includes this motto, as well as the golden rule and other core corporate principles. They're required to carry this card in their pockets every day like a lucky rabbit's foot. It reminds them to truly live by those principles.

I was so impressed by this dedication that I asked the manager for one of the cards. Even today, I carry it in my pocket whenever I perform. Even though the card wasn't intended for me, it's helped me immensely. Before I learned this principle, I thought that it was simply enough to be ultrapolite. I used to go overboard trying to be proper, in hopes that it would make me look refined. In the past, I'd say things like: "It's been a distinct honor speaking with you" and "I apologize profusely" and "May I prevail upon you to help me with this?" What I didn't realize was that this cautious language was actually lowering my status. Now I aim for equality. You can too. Speak with others the way you'd like to be spoken to.

UNIVERSAL EQUALITY

I am reminded of my hero, Austrian magician Max Malini, who was commanded to perform magic for King Edward VII of England. Before his show, Malini's colleagues briefed him on the proper protocol for addressing the king. "Don't forget to call the king Your Royal and Sacred Majesty," they warned. Also: "Walk backward in the king's presence" and "Drop to your knees when he addresses you."

Malini, though, was so proud of himself that he had no intention of following those rules of etiquette. When he met the king, Malini delighted him and Queen Alexandra with sleight-of-hand tricks using cards, coins, pencils, and other small props. The king said, "Very clever, Mr. Malini. Very clever indeed." Instead of answering in the expected manner, Malini replied, "Much obliged, Royal Mister." The king laughed at this unorthodox response. He asked Malini if he'd care to smoke a cigar. Malini gruffly said, "You bet."

Malini wrote about this experience in an article entitled "How I Mystified King Edward" (*Pearson's Weekly*, 1906): "It is quite a mistake to imagine that Royal personages are more difficult to entertain—I mean from an entertainer's point of view—than are plain Mr. And Mrs. So-and-so."

Instead of bowing in subservience, Malini assumed an attitude of universal equality. This attitude helped propel him to the upper echelons of high society, enabling him to perform for President Theodore Roosevelt, J. P. Morgan, Alexander Graham Bell, and the emperor of Japan, among many other notable people. He treated big names as if he and they were both on the same level. Soon enough, Malini himself was granted entry into their circles.

Some of the best magicians in the world have adapted a similar attitude. And you can too. You deserve to be treated with as much dignity as the most admired person you know.

If you still have doubts about your new confident self, get ready for a large awakening. The next section introduces a technique that'll help remove any discomfort you may still have in approaching others.

HOLD A STARING CONTEST

Among silverback gorillas (the world's largest primates), only the dominant male is permitted to stare at other gorillas. The stare is the way in which the leader asserts his authority over the group. The same holds true with humans: dominant people are permitted to stare, while subordinates are intimidated into looking away. This is a learned response—both for primates and humans—but it can be unlearned relatively simply.

As children, we were taught that staring is rude, and most of us have learned that lesson well. For our purposes here, we need to unlearn that bit of etiquette. Here's an exercise to practice: stare at a stranger and refuse to shift your gaze. Your sole intention in this exercise is to win by making the other person look away. It sounds a little crazy, I know. But try it. When you are walking down the street, look at the eyes of each person walking toward you and don't break your gaze under any circumstance. Some people will walk by without noticing. Others will look at you, and then look away. And others will keep staring back at you. Remember the rule: Don't break the gaze.

This is an authority-building exercise that you can easily practice in your daily life. Since I've suggested that you start with strangers in public places, you have nothing to lose (except teeth, if you're staring at someone's girlfriend). Once you feel comfortable staring at a single stranger, try the same experiment with a friend or coworker. However, this time, I want you to stare at a specific location on her face. As you look at your colleague's face, draw your gaze to a spot just above the bridge of the nose (some people call this the "third eye"). You can talk to her as usual, but keep your gaze constant upon this spot. Important: Do not shift your eyes back and forth to look at each of her eyes. Rather, stare at the "third eye" as intently as possible, trying to penetrate through to the back of her skull. You will know that you've reached the correct degree of intensity when she starts to feel uncomfortable and looks away. Bingo! In that moment, you've just gained temporary authority status.

OVERCOMING STAGE FRIGHT

Now that you feel more confident staring at a single person, you should be able to easily walk in front of a group. Right? Or maybe not. Perhaps you still feel stage fright. "I can deal with one person," you're probably thinking, "but bunches of people shut me down."

If you feel this way, you're not alone. It's okay to feel anxiety. But the way that you deal with that anxiety will make all the difference.

Instead of thinking, "What if I fail?" think "What if I succeed?" Instead of worrying if people are going to laugh *at* you, have fun yourself and you'll find that they laugh *with* you.

Before I step in front of a group, I make silly talk with people waiting with me off to the side. The things I say at that moment are pretty ridiculous. Things like, "After the show I'm gonna eat a big sticky sundae" or "Little do they know I'm not wearing underwear." Nonsensical comments like these make me feel happy and relaxed when I walk onstage.

Of course, the problem of stage fright isn't limited to the minutes before you appear in front of a group. People begin to feel pressure days in advance—when they first find out that they have to give a speech. Anticipation kills them.

Instead of torturing yourself days before a presentation, use your time to plan out a script, and then practice it anywhere you can. Always out loud, and preferably in front of other people. Remember Maxim 4: Practice, Practice, Practice. Drop snippets of your presentation into your daily conversations so that you begin to feel comfortable saying them. It doesn't much help to practice silently. When you speak the words out loud, you condition your mouth and facial muscles to remember what it feels like to produce the new sounds.

Will you still feel nervous after becoming comfortable with your material? Probably. But you can use those nerves to your advantage. Think of fear as a positive indicator. If you're not nervous before a performance, something is probably wrong. The key is never to fight the way your body naturally reacts.

When you're expected to speak, your body will pump out adrenaline and cortisol into your bloodstream. It's the fight or flight response made chemical, and you have no control over this—it's a prehistoric survival mechanism. These stimulants race through your body and make you breathe quickly and sweat. You can't totally control your body's natural response to stress. You can only control how your mind reacts to this response.

My friend Rabbi Brian Zachary Mayer frequently uses this quote in his lecturing: "The proper response to the inevitable is relaxation."

Remember, your body is going to pressure you. You know that. That's its natural reaction to being in an unnatural situation. Don't fight it. *Let* your body become nervous, but then *use* that nervousness to your benefit. Your reflexes will sharpen. Your eyesight will strengthen. Your face will be aglow. You will look alive.

Think of yourself as a rodeo bronco demanding release from the gate. Compared to all of the passively seated audience members, you'll be the liveliest person in the room. Your unbounded energy will also make you more attractive, although you may not feel that way inside.

TRAINING AT THE CINEMA

Here's a technique that you may find helpful in building your confidence. The next time you go to a movie theater, walk to the front and stand there. Face all of the people who are waiting for the movie to start. Don't say anything. Don't rush to find your seat. You may feel uncomfortable, but pretend that you are looking for someone. In fact, you are training yourself to feel comfortable standing in front of a group.

While in front of the moviegoers, begin breaking down the concept of "audience" into its smallest parts. Remember, each person looking at you is just another person. Say it with me slowly. Just. Another. Person.

Stop thinking of the audience as an ocean of staring eyeballs. Instead, remind yourself that each pair of eyeballs is connected to a regular person. Someone who wakes up in the morning, brushes his teeth, and goes to work. In fact, if the tables were turned, you would probably be just as intimidating to him!

Even if your audience is filled with celebrities or heads of state, remind yourself that they are just people too. They have the same kinds of thoughts and make the same kinds of decisions that you and I do. If they intimidate you, it's all in your mind.

TRUE TALES
FROM THE MILLIONAIRES' MAGICIAN

Anecdote 2
MY SIGNATURE TRICK

Before being elected mayor of New York City, Mike Bloomberg invited me into his office on Park Avenue—headquarters of Bloomberg LP. After chatting for twenty minutes about golf, memory techniques, and how to master a second language (he was studying Spanish), Bloomberg asked me to show him some magic.

I asked if he had a dollar. The billionaire chuckled and said, "Have *I* got a dollar? I've got quite a few!" We both laughed as he handed me a single dollar bill from his pocket.

I slowly and deliberately displayed the bill to him and called attention to the secretary of the Treasury's signature at the bottom. The name read Laurence Summers. Without a single false move, I waved my hand over that signature and magically transformed it into the signature of Bloomberg himself—Michael R. Bloomberg. The ink changed visually in front of his eyes.

He rubbed the bill with his thumb and was delighted to see that his signature had permanently been printed on his own bill—real U.S. currency. At first, he challenged me to change it back, but I countered, "Are you kidding? That's a collector's item. The next time I come to your office, I want to see that in a frame on your wall!"

That's where it hangs to this day.

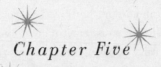

Chapter Five

PREPARE YOUR BODY AND MIND FOR THE BIG MOMENT

NOW THAT YOU'VE PREPARED yourself mentally, you're almost ready to walk in front of the crowd. However, you can only perform at your peak ability when your body's as prepared as your mind. Before every performance, I follow a regimen of physical warm-ups. These include facial stretches, voice exercises, pressure-point manipulation, and breathing. In this section, I'll teach you my personal regimen. You don't have to follow it exactly. You can pick and choose from it like a salad bar. However, once you've decided which warm-ups you like best, always follow them in the same order. An unchanging ritual offers certainty and calmness before you start speaking.

VOICE

Just like we all have bad hair days, we also have bad voice days. You know the ones. No matter how hard you try, everything comes out pinched. It's not that you're nervous. It's that you didn't tune up. Vocalists call their bodies and throats their "instruments." Your body is your instrument, and it requires regular tuning just like a piano.

What to Drink Before a Presentation

The first crucial step in preparing your voice is to drink water. *A lot* of water. Before every show, I drink a liter bottle of spring water. Pure water hydrates every cell in your body and helps make your skin radiate a healthy glow. More important, water relaxes your throat, making your voice more resonant. The moist environment eliminates any resistance that is presented by a dry throat and enables you to produce a richer, more pleasant-sounding tone. On top of that, it'll *feel* good too. You'll feel the resonation and reverberation of vocal tones more distinctly in your chest and nasal area. This helps you produce a better-quality sound.

Oh yes, remember to leave a little time to visit the restroom before the curtain goes up.

The Lion Pose

The next step is to loosen up the muscles around your throat and mouth. Do this by performing the Lion Pose, familiar to yoga practitioners. It's easy, especially since there's no need to twist your body into a pretzel. This pose focuses on the face and throat and helps release tension that builds up in these areas.

Sit erect, either in a chair or cross-legged on the floor. Close your eyes and mouth and rest your hands on your knees. Clench your hands into fists. Now deeply inhale, and then exhale forcefully through the mouth. As you release your breath, open your eyes as wide as possible, simultaneously opening your mouth and sticking your tongue out as far as possible. Stretch the muscles around your face, mouth, and eyes to their maximum. Fix your gaze at the tip of your nose and stretch your fingers straight out from your knees. Inhale and return to starting position, closing your eyes, mouth, and fists. Relax your face completely. Repeat this exercise three times.

In addition to being a marvelous technique for preventing and heal-

ing sore throats, the Lion Pose also helps strengthen your vocal apparatus. Remember to breathe smoothly and deeply as you extend your
tongue. Three repetitions will help prepare your voice before your next
presentation.

Hum a Tune

Usually we hum with our lips shut. Try it now. Hum "Twinkle Twinkle Little Star." Okay, that's enough. See how your lips are shut? Now hum it
again with your mouth open. You probably felt the location of the sound
production shift from your nose (the first time) to your throat (the second
time). Both of these areas are important when warming up.

When you hum with your lips shut, work to create larger vibrations
around your mouth and nose. Hum the whole song, remembering to inhale through your nostrils. By the end of the song, the muscles around
your mouth and nose may feel ticklish. That's perfect. It means you've
awakened them.

Next, hum with your mouth open. In reality, this is singing, but instead of lyrics, sing the sound *aah* or *ee*. Really open up your throat as you
do this. I always do this exercise in my lowest register, in as deep a voice as
possible, while still keeping the melody. At the end of this song, your
throat will be as alive as your mouth and facial muscles. The tuning process is almost done.

Tongue Twisters

Baseball players swing two bats when they are in the on-deck circle for a
specific reason: when they step up to the plate, they throw one away, and
the one they're left with feels light in comparison. Tongue twisters before
a presentation serve the same purpose for your mouth. By challenging
your lips and tongue before you walk onstage, the actual lines you need to
say will seem easy.

Here's a tongue twister that I learned from Phil Stewart, my acting coach at Horace Greeley High School in Chappaqua. Ever since, I've used it before thousands of performances. It was sung by Gene Kelly and Donald O'Connor in the movie "Singin' in the Rain."

Moses supposes his toeses are roses, but Moses supposes erroneously.

Here are several tips that will make this tongue twister effective for you. Note the word "toeses" is just a way of forcing the word "toes" to rhyme with everything else. When we'd use this phrase before musicals, the entire cast would sing and act it out as a rap song: "Moses supposes / his toeses / are roses / but Moses / supposes / erro-neous-ly."

Chant this loudly. Tongue twisters are meaningless when they're mumbled. Be sure to hit every syllable in each word. Mr. Stewart used to remind us of the *t* at the end of the word "but." The *t* sound helps to enliven the tongue even further.

Stretch your mouth as wide as you can for each word. Develop a habit of opening your mouth and fully forming each of the sounds. When you practice, you may feel you're making silly faces. That's because you are pushing yourself to an extreme. When you speak normally, your mouth will automatically adjust to the proper range of movement, and nobody will feel that your speech or facial expressions are affected.

Exaggerate Your Lines

Here's one final method that has helped me enormously. Say your opening line over and over, exaggerating the way that you say it in a different way each time. The opening lines of my show *Chamber Magic* are: "Good evening, and welcome. Tonight I'm going to show you how easy it is to read minds."

Let's see how many different ways we can say the same lines.

- **angry, raspy voice**
- **high-pitched, giggling voice**

· **Donald Duck voice**
· **slow and deep voice, like an old record player on a slow speed**
· **rising voice after each phrase, as if asking a question**

There are many more options available. Run through two or three that you like before you begin your presentation. This exercise also serves the same purpose as the second baseball bat. Since you've played with your opening lines in such a silly manner, it'll feel easy and natural to speak them with your normal voice. Despite the fact that I've spoken the same opening lines thousands of times in my performance, I still perform this exercise before every show. It soothes me to know that the first words out of my mouth will be easy to say. Give it a try. I'm certain that you will find the same to be true.

BREATHING

Breathing exercises can awaken your senses, increase your creativity, and make you more alert. I practice two exercises before every performance. If you follow this same routine, you'll feel more relaxed before walking in front of a group, and your mind will function more rapidly and efficiently. In many ways, these exercises give you a high without the need for any artificial stimulants. Breathing properly will increase the oxygen flow to your brain and increase the clarity with which you experience the world around you.

Most people do not breathe correctly. Do you? Here's one way to test yourself. Lie on your back. Put one hand on your chest and the other hand on your stomach. Now take several breaths. If your chest hand moves up and down more broadly than your stomach hand, then you aren't filling your lungs up completely. You're depriving your body of oxygen.

Three Pockets of Air

Here's the first breathing exercise that you can do before any presentation. If you work in an office, find a private corner or a room where you
won't be distracted. Stand with your feet shoulder-width apart. Drop
your arms to your sides, palms facing forward. Take a deep breath, all the
way down to your stomach. Your abdomen should expand. Hold for one,
two, three beats. You're going to layer another inhalation on top of the
one you just took, so don't exhale yet. Swing both arms up and assume a
crucifix position as you take a second breath. Your rib cage stretches to
provide extra space on the sides of each lung. Hold one, two, three beats.
You're going to layer one more inhalation on top of the last two. Reach
both arms up to the ceiling as you take a third breath. This last breath
fills the top of each lung with oxygen. Your lungs are now filled to capac-
ity. It's like you stuffed air into three pockets within your lungs—bottom,
sides, and top. Hold again for one, two, three beats. Exhale slowly and
gently lower your hands to the starting position. Repeat this exercise two
or three times.

If you actually got out of your chair and tried this exercise, right now
you should feel a natural buzz. It's extraordinary how our bodies are
equipped with everything we need to put ourselves in a peak performance
state.

Rapid-Ready Breathing

I call this exercise Rapid-Ready Breathing because it's quick, and because it readies you for any presentation. Consider it a way to pump
yourself up before you make your appearance. I always use it immediately before walking onstage. You won't look funny doing this one, so
there's no need to retire to a private room or corner. It's easy. Close your
lips so that your mouth is shut. Rapidly inhale three times through your
nostrils. These should be short and quick inhalations. Stack each inhala-

tion on top of the last, without exhaling in between. After the third inhalation, exhale slowly through your mouth. Repeat this two or three
times.

Be sure that the length of your exhalation is a little longer than the
length of your inhalations. Exhalations are what allow you to remove tox-
ins with your breath. Test it out right now. Count how many seconds it
takes you to inhale during the three rapid inhalations, and then count
how many seconds it takes to exhale. Train yourself to make your exhalations slightly longer than your inhalations (not just in this exercise, but in
everyday life too). That's the proper rhythm for breathing: exhaling
longer than you inhale.

There are many other breathing exercises available. These are the two
that I've found to be most effective and easiest to practice before a show.
They have helped me feel keenly alert for many years. Use them whenever
you want a burst of energy—first thing in the morning, before a presentation, before a meeting, or anytime you need it!

PRESSURE-POINT MANIPULATION

Acupressure is approximately five thousand years old and is believed to
have originated in ancient China. Although acupressure is no longer
commonly used as the sole treatment for medical ailments, it is an easy
and safe technique that you can practice on yourself. I use it before every
show to rev myself up naturally.

There are hundreds of pressure points throughout our bodies. Each
pressure point is connected to a specific function or area in the human
body. By massaging certain spots, you can send energy to weak or damaged areas.

I've found one pressure point to be particularly effective in increasing
alertness before giving presentations. Find it with me now. Look at the
back of your left hand. There is a V shape formed by your left thumb and
forefinger. The pressure point is located at the bottom of that V. This spot
is indicated in figure 2.

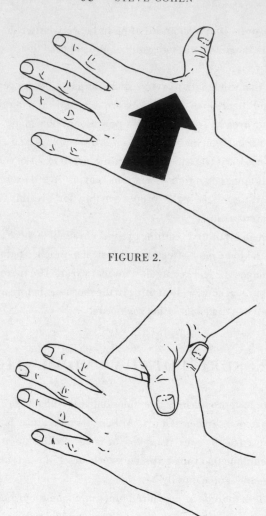

FIGURE 2.

FIGURE 3.

With your right hand, reach over the top and firmly pinch the bottom of that V with your right thumb and forefinger. Aim for the lowest part of the V, not the webby skin at the top. Refer to figure 3 for the proper position. Continue to apply pressure for thirty seconds. It may feel somewhat painful. That's natural. This pressure point helps release endorphins to the medulla of your brain. It makes you more alert. I do this before every show—thirty seconds on the left, and then thirty seconds on the right. Switch hands and repeat. Squeeze the pressure point firmly on your right hand. (Important note: Refrain from manipulating this pressure point if you are pregnant. It can damage your unborn child or cause a miscarriage.)

In addition to increasing alertness before a presentation, manipulating this pressure point will help you heal your own headaches. The next time you have anything from a minor headache to a migraine, press this pressure point for thirty to sixty seconds on each hand. You will be surprised to find that the headache will magically disappear.

When I showed this pressure point technique to Stone Phillips, anchorman for *Dateline NBC*, he told me that he felt so alert that he would begin using it before every broadcast. It can provide relief before any stressful situation—before a date, an interview, a speech, or a presentation.

FACIAL MOISTURIZER

When you begin speaking with people, they naturally look at your face. However, if you want them to continue looking at you, it helps if you look vibrant. People recognize when your face gives off a healthy glow. Picture what you look like after a great run or workout. Your skin looks alive.

Before every show, I moisturize my face to produce that glow. Although there are dozens of creams on the market, I recommend anything that contains the ingredient MSM (methylsulfonylmethane). You can find it or other moisturizers like it in organic health food stores. MSM is an organic form of sulfur that appears in living organisms. However, most people are extremely deficient in MSM, since it is volatile and evaporates from food when cooked. Creams with this ingredient replenish your skin and make your face radiate a healthy glow. Go to a health food store where they have a tester and convince yourself.

Moisturizing before you go into a meeting or presentation is easy. Keep a tube on your desk and apply it before you meet with people. If you're at someone else's office or a conference, fill a small travel container to keep in your handbag or briefcase. It takes only ten seconds to apply. Who doesn't have time for that?

Moisturizers won't give you perfect skin, but they will help you look your best.

THE EXTRA EDGE

Can you step in front of a group without preparing as I've suggested in this chapter? You most certainly can. However, thousands of performances have convinced me that you should always overprepare if you want to make a positive impression. Thorough preparation leads to thorough communication.

Control every aspect of your presentation, including what you do before you walk onstage. I use the words "walk onstage," but by now you know that this refers to anytime you step in front of another person or group of people. Prepare a mental checklist of each step in this chapter that appeals to you and methodically work your way through that list before your next presentation.

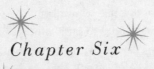

Chapter Six
HOW TO COMMAND A ROOM

NOW THAT YOU'VE PRIMED your body and mind through the exercises taught in the last two chapters, you're fully prepared to step in front of the crowd. Are you ready? This chapter will take you by the hand and teach you the best way to actually walk out and present yourself.

When you're introduced to an audience, so many thoughts rush through your head! ("Hope this goes smoothly." "How do I look?" "What should I say first?") All the while, you remember that you must establish eye contact in order to show that you are in command.

Many people choke under all the pressure and look downward, either toward their feet or at their note cards. (Note: Avoid reading verbatim from your note cards at all costs. It's very difficult to act the leader when it appears that you aren't quite sure what to say next!) On a psychological level, the act of gazing downward indicates insecurity, introspection, and a reluctance to attend to anyone but yourself. Remember, your goal is to radiate an immense amount of confidence, and to draw the audience in to meet you. To do this instantly, try what I call fanning the room.

FANNING THE ROOM

To fan the room, walk briskly from Point A (stage left) toward Point B (center stage). During this entrance, stare intently at the person sitting in the farthest seat to the right (indicated by * in figure 4). Do not break your gaze. Keep staring at this person until you have a comfortable degree of eye contact. Continue walking toward Point B, and as you come closer and closer to center stage, smoothly turn your head toward the left. By the time that you have reached Point B, your nose should be pointing toward the person sitting in the farthest seat to the left (indicated by # in figure 4). Once you are at center stage, you will have "fanned" your eyes over the entire room. Smoothly turn your head back to the right, reacknowledging the people on that side.

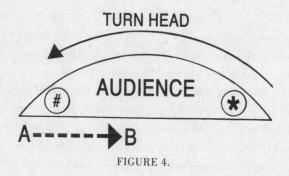

FIGURE 4.

What has this accomplished? In the brief moments that you have walked to the center of the room, you have displayed a full frontal view of your face to every person in the audience. Speakers who do not fan the room present only a partial view of their faces to certain portions of the audience. It is certainly more difficult to create a close connection with an audience of strangers when you have not given them a chance to visually check you out.

WHICH FOOT STEPS FIRST WHEN YOU WALK ONSTAGE?

Magician Vito Lupo takes this thinking further by applying a classic actor's technique. In his lectures, he offers the following advice: When entering from the left, take your first step with your right foot. When entering from the right, take your first step with your left foot.

This stage technique presents a more open view of your body when walking in front of a group. If you violate this advice, the first thing that audiences will see is your shoulder and your profile. If you follow this advice, though, the audience's first impression of you is more visually stimulating. They see a broader, frontal view of your chest, and you appear to take up more space. You appear more commanding because you are more visible.

TWO INVISIBLE STEPS

Now that you understand which foot should step forward first, you're ready to fine-tune your entrance even more. The first two steps you take should be "invisible," that is, offstage. The audience should first see you only at the moment that you take your third step. Why is this? It's difficult to launch your body forward when starting from a still position. Unlike a sports-car engine, we humans can't propel ourselves from zero to sixty in mere seconds. We need time to build up speed, energy, and momentum.

Within seconds of appearing in front of a group, you want them to know that you are a presence, a force that they can't ignore. The two invisible steps are akin to revving your engine before walking on. They ensure that your third step will be full of gusto.

You may be wondering if it's possible to combine Vito Lupo's advice with the two invisible steps to make an incredibly powerful entrance. Absolutely. Here's how to do it.

- Take two steps backward from where you will be making your entrance. This spot could be the doorway, the side of the room, or behind the edge of a curtain.
- When entering from the left, your first three steps should be right foot, left foot, right foot.
- When entering from the right, your first three steps should be left foot, right foot, left foot.

In each case, your third step will be the first one that is visible to the audience. Because three is an odd number, this cadence will automatically force you to step into view on the proper foot.

HOW TO FLOAT INTO A ROOM

At the beginning of this book, I promised that I wouldn't reveal how magicians make people float. But in this section, I'll teach you how to command instant attention by floating into a room yourself. Magicians, actors, and speakers have used this technique for many years. It is so simple and will help build your confidence as you make your entrance.

Before you step in front of an audience, take a deep breath. Fill your lungs with oxygen until they are ready to burst. Once you feel that the air has reached the top of your chest cavity, hold it in. Then, and only then, walk into the room.

This is a much more powerful entrance than if you were to walk in with your lungs deflated. Many people who haven't learned this technique walk onstage with no air in their lungs and take a quick inhalation immediately before speaking. Don't be one of those people. Before you walk on, fill your lungs with oxygen. The inhalation will increase the blood flow to your face, and you'll appear more radiant, more lively.

Once you've entered the room and start to speak, your lungs will naturally empty themselves of air. If you won't be speaking right away, however, please remember to exhale. If you hold your breath, you'll pass out before long. No matter how good your initial impression was, you won't win any points when you're carried out on a stretcher.

This breathing technique is easy to practice. Take a moment to fuel up outside the office door the next time you walk in to submit a report to your boss. Inhale fully and enter the room when your lungs are floating in your chest cavity. The audience (in this case your boss) will notice the confident glow that your face emits. You are poised to begin speaking from a position of power, not intimidation or insecurity.

OWN THE STAGE

When you speak to groups, it's important to feel like you own the stage. Your "stage" may not be a stage at all but an office, a conference room, or a classroom. No matter where you happen to be speaking, take command of that space. Say to yourself, "This is my place. I am at home here. I own it." Just like a sports team playing on its home court, you'll feel more confident, sending out a silent signal that you're in control.

This is easy when you're in a location that you've been in before, like your office or your company's conference room. There are no surprises. You know where everything is. When you're in unfamiliar territory, however, here are some steps you can take to give yourself the home court advantage.

Steps to Owning the Stage

Step 1 is to arrive early and do a walk-through of the room. I often fly in a day early just to be able to "trod the boards" prior to an event. It helps to know how the room is laid out so that you can adjust your presentation accordingly. Professional entertainers send written instructions (called a rider) in advance that specify all of the working conditions, including a floor plan. The idea is to reduce or eliminate uncertainty prior to the event. Arriving early to scout the location is a crucial stage of your preparation. Make this your motto: "No surprises."

Step 2 is to sit in the audience and look up at the performance area. Decide where you will stand. Certain areas will have better visibility and lighting. Move around from seat to seat and imagine the experience people will have when they sit in those seats. Reposition objects that obstruct people's view, or, in the case of large pillars, reposition the seats themselves.

Naturally, there are times when it's impossible to arrive early. Still, you can take ownership of the room with Step 3, which is to treat the room as your own. Move the furniture around. Reposition chairs or push a table off to the side. Ask people to rise from their chairs and stand or sit in different locations. In his book *Magic and Showmanship*, Henning Nelms wrote, "Never stress a motivation. All you need is to convince the audience that an adequate motivation exists." If you appear to have a reason for shifting people and furniture around (e.g., "You'll see this better if you stand over here"), they'll accept your request without raising an eyebrow.

DON'T HIDE BEHIND THE LECTERN

Here is a valuable tip: Stand in front of the table, not behind it. When you stand behind a desk or table, the audience only sees your upper body. Many speakers feel protected behind a lectern. They look down at their notes and keep their hands busy by gripping the podium edge. This is a critical mistake, as it highlights their insecurity. If you want to own the stage, people need to be able to see you from head to toe. Step out from behind the lectern, desk, or table and you'll project a stronger message.

If you're at a meeting where everyone is seated around a table, you can make yourself more visible by simply standing up when it's your turn to speak. Don't feel rooted to your chair. Remember, it's *your* room, and you can stand up if you feel like it.

LOVE YOUR AUDIENCE

Before you step in front of a group, ask yourself, "Why am I here?" The best entertainers know that the answer is, "I'm here for the audience." The audience doesn't exist to satisfy you. Rather, you exist to delight and inform them.

When you step onstage, don't think, "Here I am!" Instead, think, "There you are! Wow, you came here to see me?"

This is an important shift in thinking. Beginning magicians think that magic is all about the props. When they walk onstage, they look down at those props—cards, ropes, or what have you. They lose their audiences quickly because they assume that the audience cares about what the magician cares about.

The fact is that audiences care about one thing—their own experience. It's the job of the presenter to focus on that experience, and to make it a pleasurable one.

Love your audience. I learned this from Howard Thurston, a celebrity magician in the early twentieth century. He traveled the world with a huge show, making elephants disappear. He was the real deal. Before he walked onstage, he would stand behind the curtains and say to himself, "I love my audience, I love my audience . . ." And he'd repeat it to himself over and over again before he walked on. By the time he got to center stage, he radiated love for his audience. He radiated a connection. He wasn't just performing *at* them. He wanted them to become part of the experience.

Make this your mantra before interactions with others, even before a business meeting: "I love my client" or "I love my colleagues." You'll prime yourself for a positive experience. I do this before every show. I love my audience as much as I love my wife and children.

BE GENUINE

It boils down to being genuine. People want to feel important; they want to know that they are not just another audience. I've seen many entertainers fail by stepping in front of a group and reciting lines that were obviously memorized. If the audience thinks they're hearing the same pitch that you give everybody, then they won't think that you're speaking to them or their needs. They will sense that they are being spoken *at*.

Early in my career I worked as a magic consultant to TV magician David Blaine. One day when we were on tour in New Orleans, he shoved a deck of cards toward me and asked me to show him a trick. Blaine loved the trick that I showed him but hated my presentation. He said that it sounded too rehearsed. He told me, "Don't prepare what you are going to say. People should feel like you're talking to them for the first time."

From that moment forward, I decided that I would always know what I wanted to say in a general framework but not recite it word for word. If I sound stilted, people would think I overprepared to talk to them.

If you work in the service business, let your genuineness show through. Just like an entertainer, you recite the same or similar information over and over again. To prevent yourself from sounding mechanical, remind yourself that the people you are speaking to are hearing your words for the first time. Just like a stage actor, do your best to be "in the moment." You are playing a character—yourself—who has never said those words before. Let your script drop away and look at your audience dead in the eyes. When you consciously recognize that there are live people in front of you, the words come out sounding much fresher. Your words seem to be in response to the circumstances that you are both facing *right now*.

How can you be more real and in the moment? Remember this phrase: Acting is *reacting*. When people talk to you, don't spend any time concocting a clever response. Instead, listen to them—really listen to them. Your most genuine responses will pop right out of you when you listen to what people say, and how they say it.

As a magician, I'm always asked the same questions: "How did you first get started in magic?" "How old were you when you did your first trick?" "Do you know how to make the Statue of Liberty disappear?" and so on. I have pat answers for all of these questions, but I very rarely rely on them word for word. Instead, I play with the phrasing each time I respond, saying them each a little differently every time. This helps keep the answers fresh and natural-sounding.

Try this today. When someone asks you a question that you've answered hundreds of times, stop. Answer it differently. This change can be as minor as shifting the order of your sentences. Or you could try saying something entirely new. Either way, you can be sure that your response will be more genuine and "in the moment." You will be reacting to the reality of your present situation and not reliving the same one over and over again.

MAKE EYE CONTACT

Audiences look where you look. This is one of the fundamentals of magic. If you look down, they'll look down. If you look up, they'll look up. Need proof? I bet that when two or more people on a city street look upward to the top of a building, you look up too. You think, "If it's interesting to them, it'll be interesting to me."

What happens if you look directly at the audience? Obviously, they can't look back at themselves (that would leave them cross-eyed!), so they have no choice but to look at you. Eye contact is critical in building a connection with others, and there are some specifics that you should remember every time you stand in front of a group. I owe my knowledge of these following stagemanship techniques to Spain's master magician, Juan Tamariz.

1. **Use imaginary strings.** Pretend that imaginary strings connect your eyes to the eyes of each person in the group. Keep them tight by returning the gaze of people looking at you. Don't allow the centers to sag, because if they sag too far, the strings will break.

2. **Reestablish eye contact.** If a thread breaks, work quickly to retie it. Do this with inattentive audience members by walking toward them. Move closer and direct your speech to them; your proximity will bring them back into focus. And only direct your gaze to others after the defectors are back on board.

3. **Hold longer than expected.** When you look at the eyes of someone in your group, lock your gaze with that person for longer than you normally would. Most speakers are nervous when standing in front of others and allow their eyes to flit about from person to person. I recommend you instead hold your gaze on specific people for longer than they would expect. Direct your entire talk to them personally for about ten or fifteen seconds. This attention makes them feel important, as if nobody else is in the room. Politicians do this, entertainers do this, and you can easily do this too.

4. **Locate key people.** If there are hundreds of people in your group, you obviously can't spend so much time on every person. With larger audiences, locate key people who are attentive and responsive. Make sure to select people who are spread out in different areas of the audience. Then, shift your gaze from key person to key person. The people surrounding each of those key people will feel your genuine attention. Don't make the mistake often made by beginning speakers, who simply aim their head toward clusters of people. Without eye contact, it is difficult to build trust. Consciously locate key people and speak to them as if you are the only two people in the room.

5. **Check the other person's eye color.** In one-on-one situations, make a conscious effort to check the color of the other person's eyes. Are they brown, blue, green, hazel, gray? Are there any flecks of color? This simple observation forces you to make eye contact. Later, if you find yourself drifting during a conversation, recheck the person's eye color. This serves as a handy way to remind yourself to retie the broken invisible string.

FACE FRONT

Never turn your back to the audience. This is a cardinal rule for actors, magicians, and all public speakers. When you turn your back, you can't see the audience, and they can't see you. All eye contact is broken. Your words will sound muffled, and you'll lose any rapport that you had established. The only time I turn my back during a magic show is when I want to emphasize that I can't see what the audience is doing (such as when they're selecting a card or drawing a secret picture). Otherwise, I make a conscious effort to face front and keep the performer-audience relationship alive.

If you are completely surrounded by people, rotate your body frequently so that you only show your back to each group for a brief time. Zigzag your focus from group to group around the room, instead of moving in a predictable, clockwise pattern. They'll never know where you're going to look next. This technique makes audiences anticipate the next moment that you shower them with attention.

45-DEGREE RULE

There is a proper and improper way to stand when addressing a group. It's called the 45-Degree Rule. Stand up and try this right now so you understand how it works. First I'll teach you how to stand improperly, and then you'll learn how to correct it. Stand with both feet pointing forward. Shift your weight to your right foot. Now shift your weight to your left foot. Keep alternating your weight back and forth: left, right, left, right. If there's anyone watching you in the room right now, they might begin to feel seasick! When your feet are parallel, you have no choice but to rock like a boat every time you redistribute your weight. This is clearly the improper way to stand. Audiences can't focus on a moving target. Constant rocking also makes you look nervous and uncomfortable.

It's easy to correct this with the 45-Degree Rule. Point your right foot forward and move your left heel to the back of your right heel. Point your left toes so they're positioned at a 45-degree angle to the left of center. Now try to shift your weight to the right as before. Guess what? You can't do it without falling over. The position you are currently standing in doesn't allow you to shift your weight. You're anchored to the floor with a firm foundation. Later, if your right leg gets tired of supporting your body's weight, make a single shift by reversing the stance. Position your left foot so that it points forward. Move your right heel back to touch the rear of the left heel and point your right toes 45 degrees to the right of center.

You can test your foot position with the Newspaper Test. Fold a sheet of newspaper diagonally to create a 45-degree angle. As shown in figure 5, place the center of one heel at the triangle point. Align your other foot along the diagonal fold. If you want to test the other side, flip the sheet of newspaper over and set up your feet again in the opposite orientation.

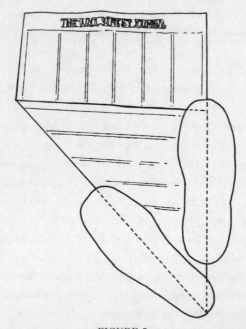

FIGURE 5.

LEAN FORWARD

Once you've established your foot position, lean your entire body forward toward the audience. This creates a more active posture that signals enthusiasm and energy to the audience. When you lean in toward people, they will often reciprocate and lean in toward you. This indicates their interest in your message.

MOVE MORE GRACEFULLY

I saw a cartoon that showed a house cat looking into a mirror. The reflection in the mirror, however, showed the face of a ferocious tiger! Many people fall into a similar trap. They see themselves one way, but others view them entirely differently. Do you know how your body really appears to others?

One great way to find out is to take a dance or movement class. Dance studios are lined with an entire wall of mirrors, a luxury that few people have at home. This environment will provide you with a new perspective of how you look when you move your body. Most people only observe themselves in the mirror when they are standing still. But during a dance class, you can observe how you move in comparison to the other members of your class. You will become more aware of the way you move through space. You'll also become more graceful. There is a subtle attractiveness about someone who has poise and grace.

SPEAK UP!

Every word you speak needs to be heard throughout the room. You can't connect with a crowd if they're constantly asking, "What did he say?" Aim your voice up and out, toward the top of the far wall of the room. Don't point your head down, since the floor absorbs sound. Your words will become muffled and inaudible to all but those in the front row. Imagine that a little old lady is sitting in the last row of chairs. She is hard of hearing and has her hand up to her ear. As Juan Tamariz suggests, dedicate your entire performance to her. Throughout your presentation, remind yourself of the little old lady and project your voice so that even she can hear you.

There's no need to shout. My high school drama coach proved this to me one day when he was standing in the parking lot. He was about to get into his car when he realized he had left a folder on his desk. He asked a group of students if someone would go and get the folder for him. Although he was standing one hundred feet away, it sounded as if he were whispering directly into our ears. My friend and I looked at each other and said, "Now *that's* projection!"

The secret of projecting your voice is to use your breath to support your voice as you speak. If you shout or yell, you'll strain your voice box. We don't want that. Instead, imagine that your voice originates in your abdomen or lower back (not your throat). When you inhale, your stomach should expand, and when you exhale your stomach should retract back into your body. During the exhalation, let your breath carry the sound up and out of your body in a continuous stream. The more efficiently you breathe, the more air you'll have to sustain your voice and project it to your listeners.

When you speak, relax your jaw and tongue and unclench your teeth. Any tightness in the mouth will pinch your voice and prevent you from articulating your words. Go back to chapter 5 and learn the Lion Pose, if you haven't already. I've found this stretch to be extremely helpful in producing clearer and more articulate speech.

Always attempt to make your voice fill the entire room. If you need to use a microphone because the room is large or the audience is spread out, the way you hold the microphone is extremely important. Many novices hold the microphone down in front of their chests, so it's pointing up and down. This is not the proper technique. Instead, hold the microphone directly in front of your mouth, at a 90-degree angle from your face. Refer to any professional singer and you'll see exactly how it's done. Remember: every word you speak needs to be heard throughout the room.

BE A SHOWMAN

Shakespeare wrote, "All the world's a stage, and all the men and women merely players." You may never step onto a real theater stage, but you can use the new tools you've learned in this chapter to make your presentations and speeches more dramatic and effective.

The nuts and bolts techniques in this chapter will help you on your way to becoming a real showman. This is certainly something to aspire to. When you're a showman, people will inch forward in their seats to hear what you've got to say. They won't shift their attention from your presentation, because they don't want to miss what you might say next. Showmen speak with lively language, walk with a confident gait, and deliver material with a twinkle in their eyes. You can become a showman by attending to the details outlined in this chapter, and throughout this book.

The best way to learn what works is to actually put yourself in front of a live audience and see what the audience responds to best. Experiment with the way you enter, the way you stand, the way you speak. Eventually you will find a pattern that works best for you. The more you use these techniques, the more they will become your own. After a while you won't even have to think about them, because they will be second nature. That's when you know that you have mastered the principles of showmanship.

TRUE TALES
FROM THE MILLIONAIRES' MAGICIAN

Anecdote 3
THERE'S MONEY IN SHOES

Paul Fireman, the CEO of Reebok, invited me to his sprawling Cape Cod mansion on July Fourth. When he introduced me to his guests, he joked, "Steve will have to change his name to the *Billionaires'* Magician, since there are several of you here tonight!" Everybody laughed and then shifted their eyes to me. It was do-or-die time. Lots of important people in the room. Fortunately, I had prepared a special trick for the occasion.

I borrowed two twenty-dollar bills from the guests and had the lenders record their serial numbers. And then I surprised them by ripping the two bills to shreds. I folded the small green pieces into a bundle and then made them all disappear in a burst of flames. "Your money's gone, but no need to worry," I explained.

I directed everyone's attention to a ceiling beam high overhead. A box of Reebok sneakers had been hanging there all night from a long piece of rope. I deadpanned, "Earlier this evening I spoke with Paul Fireman, and he told me a secret. He said, 'Steve, you know, *there's money in shoes!'* Let's see if he was right."

A stagehand lowered the box, and Fireman's family removed the lid themselves. Could the shredded bills have possibly been restored and transported into the box? The guests reached deep inside the toes of the sneakers and found two twenty-dollar bills, one inside each shoe. The lenders confirmed that the serial numbers were exactly the same as the bills they had offered.

Sure enough, there *is* money in shoes.

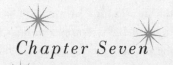

Chapter Seven

ORGANIZATION AND PRESENTATION SECRETS

THE FIFTH MAXIM OF Magic is "Be Prepared." This chapter will help you prepare the content of your presentations using some of the organizational secrets I've learned as a magician. Some of them are sneaky, like Planned Failure and Left to Right, while some are more straightforward and nitty gritty. Since you've read through the book with me this far, you're definitely ready to learn some of these useful secrets.

PLANNED FAILURE

Failure only makes the successes more exciting.
—*Chan Canasta*

If you come across as too slick, people won't want to pay attention to you for very long. I'm sure you can imagine the type: someone who knows every answer, dresses perfectly, who doesn't even appear human. Sometimes you have to intentionally show your fallibility to keep people on your side.

One of the techniques magicians use is Planned Failure. I greatly enjoy planning out my failures—in fact, I rehearse them. I believe that people want to see other people fail. And then they want to see those people overcome failure. The bigger the failure, the greater the impact when the desired outcome actually occurs.

In my show, I perform Think-a-Drink, a very old but effective trick in which I pour any beverage called for, from a single teakettle. For instance, a lady yells out "Cosmopolitan!" I pick up the kettle and immediately pour her a cosmo. A gentleman asks for a dirty martini, which comes splashing out of the spout, to his delight. A skeptical man requests single malt scotch. I pour one for him straightaway. Each spectator drinks his beverage and confirms that it's exactly what he asked for. At this point, people usually wonder where they can buy a teakettle like mine! Finally, I ask a woman to name her favorite drink. She replies, for example, "champagne." I tilt the kettle to pour, and nothing emerges. I try again, but no luck. No champagne. I apologize. The audience senses that something is not right, so I apologize and finish the trick gracefully.

Much later, after about thirty minutes have passed, I present the climax of my show—the grand finale. Emotions run high and the audience is stimulated and abuzz. I remind them about the champagne she requested: "Madam, do you still want that glass of champagne?" I pick up the teakettle one last time, tip it forward, and pour out a full glass of champagne. The audience usually shouts a collective "Yeah!" punching their fists upward into the air. The tension of my repeated failures is relieved cathartically.

Even though I am actually capable of pouring champagne the first time around, the perfect execution of this feat would hardly capture the audience's heartstrings. That's the big secret. Would you want to hear someone say "Look at me do this difficult task!" and watch him succeed every time? It is much more interesting when that person says "Look at me do this," and you watch him attempt the task incorrectly a few times. You come to your *own* conclusion that this task must be very difficult, without it being spelled out for you. After all, he has failed a few times, so it can't be all that easy, right? The successful conclusion brings closure and draws a bigger response, every time.

The psychology behind the Planned Failure strategy is diabolical. By seeing your failure, audiences want you to succeed. They come to your side. In general, we root for the underdog and hope that he prevails. It is difficult to like somebody who succeeds in every endeavor. We have more respect for people who successfully overcome adversity.

Is it possible to purposely position yourself as the underdog? Can you use Planned Failure with your clients, your boss, your date? Try thinking of ways to rehearse your failures so that people will cheer you on when you succeed.

Here is one application that I taught to a client. He works in a powerful advertising agency and delivers presentations to his clients regularly. In his presentations, he often projects PowerPoint slides onto a large screen so that everyone in the conference room is able to see. The problem with using a PowerPoint presentation is that *everyone else* in the business community does too. In order to break the monotony, I suggested that he use Planned Failure as follows. Right before he reaches a critical point of his presentation, he announces that the next PowerPoint slide is of major importance. He really builds it up, explaining that the next point will tie everything together. He clicks his remote control to advance, but nothing happens. The image on the screen remains the same. He clicks again, aiming the remote directly at his laptop. No luck. Another click? Nothing but frustration. He looks flustered and apologizes to his client, saying that he is embarrassed, because this was supposed to be his most important point. He claims that he will give it one last try. He aims the remote control, presses the button, and this time—voilà! The slide advances successfully and he flashes a triumphant smile.

You'd better believe that people are going to pay attention to what he has to say next. He successfully built up their expectations and, simultaneously, their sympathy. Little do they know that my client was simply pressing the mute button on the remote control over and over. That, plus a few acting skills, made his Planned Failure entirely believable.

One tip—make sure that you don't use this technique more than once with the same client. Even we magicians make sparing use of Planned Failures. Its overuse screams "Setup!" to those on the receiving end, and you will be dismissed as a sideshow charlatan.

A situation that does not warrant Planned Failures is evidenced in the following story. When well-known memory expert and fellow magician Harry Lorayne was ten years old, he was introduced to a pretty teenage girl. Heart aflutter, he didn't know what to say, so he decided to show her a card trick. She took a card, returned it, and shuffled the deck. Before Harry could continue, the girl said, "If you can find my card, I'll give you a kiss!" Harry's mind was racing, thinking over the most impressive way to locate her card. He decided to deliberately show her the wrong card, and then magically transform it into the correct one. When he showed her the wrong card, he announced, "This is your card." Although he was ready to secretly swap that card for hers, she stopped him cold and laughed. "You're wrong," she said as she turned and walked away. No resolution, and more important, no kiss.

The lesson here is to use Planned Failures with people who respect you. Unlike the teenage girl, they won't walk away, but will give you benefit of the doubt until they see you succeed.

PAUSE FOR THE CAUSE

When you speak to people, they often split their attention. Half is on what you're saying, and half is on what they'll say next.

Theatrical performers, though, use a simple technique to capture people's full attention.

Silence.

In the theater, it's called a dramatic pause. After you say something important, stop. Don't rush forward to the next point. Let your message sink in.

Imagine what happens in people's heads during a pause. The external stream of information—your voice—ceases, and listeners can focus only on their internal thoughts. It's as if their silent voice says, "What happened? Oh, I'm all alone now. Let me think about what I just heard."

Psychology studies have demonstrated the effects of "recency" upon our memories. In general, people are more capable of remembering things they have experienced *most recently*. If I were to read you a long list of groceries, for instance, you'd be most likely to remember the last item or two that you heard. A dramatic pause works for the same reason. People remember what they heard most recently. The silence you offer during the pause allows them to contemplate your message with no distractions.

Remind yourself to stop after you've said something important. Silence creates texture in your presentations. Musicians know that music isn't just about the notes, it's about the rests between those notes. The absence of sound draws people in.

ENGAGE THE FIVE SENSES

If you are a beer drinker, then you've probably performed the following ritual hundreds of times. After pouring yourself a beer, you raise your glass and clink it against your friend's. Cheers! Then you guzzle down your ale and enjoy the inevitable buzz. This ritual is part of the enjoyment of drinking beer. Have you ever considered why?

Four of the senses are automatically involved when drinking beer. Your eyes see the foam on top of the beer. Your nose smells the unmistakable scent of hops. Your tongue tastes the beverage. And your fingers feel the cool moisture on the side of the glass. The only sense that is not involved is the sense of sound. However, when you clink the glasses together, your ears also become involved in the process. The clink enables you to engage all of your five senses. It becomes a fully sensorial experience that you want to repeat over and over again (hopefully on different days).

As a magician, I've learned that you can enhance the audience's experience of a magic trick by forcing them to use more senses. By its very nature, magic is clearly a visual art. You need to be able to see what the magician is doing, or there is little point. However, visual demonstrations alone are not enough to keep people interested. Through the introduction of sound and touch, audiences become more involved in the experience. (If I can think up a way to invoke the senses of smell and taste, I'd include those too!) Let's look at an example of how this works in a magic trick, and then we'll see how you can apply this principle in your own presentations.

In my left hand I'm holding three silver dollars. I stack them together and silently place them into my right fist. When I open the fist, the coins have vanished. Good trick, right? Sure, but here's how I've improved it to increase the audience's interest level. First, instead of silently placing the coins into my fist, I toss them inside. The coins jingle against one another as they land in my right hand. Then, I ask an audience member to reach forward and tightly hold my right wrist ("so nothing can fly up my sleeve"). When my hand opens, the three coins have vanished! Now that's magic. It is so much more convincing than the first example because the audience can hear and feel what is happening—not just see. By the way, I've practiced this same trick with chocolate coins so that the audience would be able to *smell* the coins right before they vanish. I gave up on this, though, by making the chocolate coins disappear a different way—by eating them!

How can you use this insight in your own life? Always think of ways that you can incorporate more than one sense when you present your ideas. Instead of simply *saying* something, *show* a diagram as you say it. Let people *hold* something. And one of my favorites: prepare a distinctive *scent* in the room where you will be presenting your ideas. Hotels do this, boutiques do this, and you can do this too, to invigorate the people who come to your office or place of work. I do this before every show. Here's my secret.

Go to a natural foods store and buy a spray bottle of pure rose water. It's made from the distilled water of roses, and it smells heavenly. Make sure that you buy one hundred percent pure rose water, not synthetic rose oil and water with added preservatives. Before a meeting in your office, spray a few puffs of rose water in the air. Roses have the highest electrical content of all flowers and raise the negative ions in the room. Most people who live in cities are surrounded by positive ions that strip their energy away. The negative ionic charge from rose water will make people feel more alert and stimulated—just the right mood to listen to your presentation. If you don't believe me, go to a natural foods store and spray one puff in front of your face. You'll feel energized and more alive almost instantly.

If you're a man, don't be concerned about the feminine connotations of roses. Everyone loves the smell of flowers, and roses are the most beloved of all. Keep a small spray bottle in your office drawer and lightly spray the room before your next meeting. It works, so try it.

Here's another example of how to stimulate more than one sense. A patient was at her doctor's office to discuss her osteoporosis. The doctor verbally explained how her bones would weaken further if she did not take a new medicine. The patient didn't understand clearly. There are different stages of osteoporosis, and his description of them wasn't making complete sense. The doctor saw that he wasn't getting through to the patient, and he reached behind his desk to remove a model that depicts bone structure. The model was all dusty, because he rarely used it. He allowed the patient to manipulate the bones herself so that she could see how her skeleton would deteriorate if she didn't take the medicine. Once he allowed her to handle this visual aid, the patient understood perfectly what he was trying to explain.

Are your visual aids gathering dust too? Like the doctor, we have many visual aids at our disposal. How many times have you neglected to use them? Remember, our minds think in pictures. Always do anything you can to add more sensory stimulation to your message, and people will absorb it more rapidly and more thoroughly. Just keep away from Power-Point as your sole visual aid. It tends to dull the senses, not invigorate them.

LEFT TO RIGHT

This is one of my most guarded psychological secrets. This presentation skill works on a subconscious level, and audiences never even know that you're consciously working to influence them. The best thing about this secret is that it is based on ingrained patterns that we have followed without thinking since we were very young.

If I were to present you with the following series of letters you would probably feel confused:

P O N M L K

However, the next series of letters would make you nod your head in agreement:

K L M N O P

What is the point here? The same series of letters feels "right" when they are ordered from left to right, but feels awkward when ordered from right to left. This is based on the psychological principle of cognitive dissonance, a phenomenon that refers to the discomfort felt when there's a discrepancy between what you already know or believe and newly furnished information. In Western culture, we read from left to right and top to bottom. From a very young age, we are taught that this is the only correct way to read, so we accept it as fact on a subconscious level. It becomes so obvious that there is no need to even think or talk about it! Anything that contradicts this accepted format, however, stands out like a sore thumb.

How can you incorporate this principle to lull people into your way of thinking? When you stand in front of a group, your audience's left is to your right. So, the most basic way to work from left to right is to stand on your right side (their left) of the room when you begin your talk. As you continue speaking, move toward the center, and when you are wrapping things up, walk to your left side of the room. This simple choreography helps frame the beginning, middle, and end of your presentation in an easily remembered format. After everyone has gone home, your audience will think back to what you presented, and it will make a certain kind of implicit sense. You can attribute this sense of satisfaction, rationality, or well-being to the simple movement from left to right that corresponded with the exposition of your speech.

You can engender a similar sense of instinctive correctness by employing a pattern of hand gestures while you're speaking.

Do this right now so that you can feel exactly what I mean. First, stand up and look at yourself in a mirror. Put your right hand on your hip, so your right arm is bent at the elbow. Now hold your left hand up and cross it over to your right side. You can extend your left pointer finger if you like.

Now pretend that you are talking to someone. Every time that you want to emphasize a point you are making, swing your left hand to the left. From your listener's perspective your hand moved briskly from left to right, which subconsciously feels right (remember?). The gesture "goes with the grain" of the thought or idea, and thus is met with no psychological resistance by the listener.

You can obtain the opposite result by switching all the rights and lefts in the above paragraph. In other words, place your left hand on your left hip and gesture with your right hand. This time, swing your right hand from your left to your right. This gesture will feel less comfortable to your listener, and on a subconscious level, it will make him doubtful or suspicious of the corresponding words.

You can also apply this intuitive sense of "correctness" to the overall structure of your presentation, by organizing your information to conform to our natural thought patterns.

SERIES OF THREE

Hit 'em over the head, tie 'em in a knot, and get off.
—Advice from legendary Coney Island magician Al Flosso

Whether you are aware of it or not, your life is governed by the "series of three." When you were a small child, this psychological principle was hardwired into your innermost psyche. Think back. All of your favorite stories had a beginning, a middle, and an end. There were three bears, and Aladdin was granted three wishes. Running races began with "Ready, set, go." When you needed to pick up something heavy, you learned to "lift on three—one, two, three, lift!" And if you believe in Christianity, you learned about the Trinity.

Something just "feels right" when we hear or present information in chunks of three. Surely this feeling of comfort arises from familiarity. And since we are used to this triplicate format, we respond favorably when information is presented to us this way. When information is delivered in two parts, we expect or anticipate a third. If this never comes, we react unfavorably, as if something is missing. Likewise, when there are four parts, we react unfavorably because there was too much information provided.

Magicians utilize this comforting rhythm to condition the audience's expectations in such a way that they miss the secret move. Not coincidentally, many magic tricks involve three objects: three cups, three rings, three ropes, three coins, three cards (think three-card monte). Most of these tricks have been constructed to create a degree of complacency after the third object is introduced. Let's look at how you can use this concept to make your own nonmagical presentations more effective.

Comedians understand the series of three (at least the funny ones do!) and assemble their jokes in the following format: Joke 1—the setup, Joke 2—the build, Joke 3—the payoff. And, as long as the jokes are funny, audiences respond to this pattern predictably: first they chuckle, then they laugh solidly, and finally they have a good belly laugh.

Talk-show legend Johnny Carson qualified this lesson on an episode of *The Tonight Show*. During his monologue, as was often the case, Carson related jokes in rapid succession. The audience reacted exactly as I described above. But after the third joke, Carson told a fourth—to try and "top" himself. The result? Silence, on national television. And do you know what he said? "I should have stuck to the rule of three."

Whenever you present information to people, organize it into chunks of three. If you offer up two bits of advice, people will feel that you've left them hanging. They'll be waiting for the third item. Likewise, four is just one too many.

When I give an impromptu magic performance at a party or bar, I present three tricks. Although the informal show seems to be off the cuff, it's been carefully planned out to represent a beginning, a middle, and an end.

For my more formal shows, I present nine major tricks (that's three times three). The show is divided into three parts: a beginning, a middle,

and an end. Each of those parts is subdivided into three tricks. Each part
of the show builds theatrically, and the show itself is built on sound psychological structure.

Although I'm sure you've heard it before, this classic formula works
wonders to provide perfect structure to your own presentations:

1. Think of three major points that you want to communicate. Let's
   call them A, B, and C.
2. Organize them so that C has the most impact among the three
   topics.
3. Tell your audience what you are going to tell them: "Today I am going to discuss three major points—A, B, and C."
4. Tell your audience about A, B, and C.
5. Conclude by reminding your audience what you told them: "Today I
   introduced you to A. I clarified B, and we discussed the importance
   of C."

In addition to presenting three topics, your presentation itself consists of
three parts, which "feels right," as we discussed above. More complex
stories such as novels, movies, and many sitcom television programs go
one step further and offer "triple trilogies." In this format, there are three
individual stories, each of which has a beginning, a middle, and an end.
At the end, all three threads intermingle and tie together the separate
story lines to create a satisfying completion to the overall story.

Now that you are consciously aware of the role that the triple trilogy
plays in storytelling, try to see how it is used in the next movie or television program you watch. Don't be a passive viewer; think about how the
screenwriter plotted out the story to present it most effectively. This may
take away some of the fun of being wrapped up in the story itself. However, I suggest that you learn from these pros. Top screenwriters are hired
for their ability to engage viewers. And that is exactly what you are working to accomplish as well—to capture your audience's attention, keep
them engaged, and finally wrap things up (notice the three parts?).

The next time you give a talk, write a letter, or present an argument (notice that again?), try organizing your presentation into three parts as described above. You will be impressed by how comfortable it feels to the listener. Since your presentation is structurally sound, you will be free to focus on the *delivery* of your material with the knowledge that your audience is listening, and on your side.

PEAKS AND VALLEYS

It is difficult to sustain high levels of interest in any topic for an extended period of time. (I'm impressed that you've read this far through the book!) We all need to take short breaks to relax, recenter, and refocus our thoughts. Most successful magic shows are designed with this in mind and contain carefully planned peaks and valleys—rich textures of emotion and excitement that highlight what the magician wants you to remember, and "lowlight" what he wants you to forget.

The peak of each mountain indicates a moment of emphasis—a moment of dramatic tension. The polar opposite of this tension is the valley—a moment of relaxation. Without these peaks and valleys (or tension and relaxation), a magic performance will appear to be monotonous and uncompelling. In a moment, you will learn how to use peaks and valleys to enhance your speaking, whether in a public forum or a private argument.

Through amusing patter, bright colors, or visually attractive props, magicians lend a great deal of importance to a certain moment (the finale of a trick, for example). When this moment has culminated, the audience is coaxed to let down their guard just enough so that the magician may perform the crucial, secret move. Indeed, the reason that you are usually unable to "catch" the secret move is because the magician performed it on the "offbeat," the moment when your mind was relaxing from the previous stimulation. As discussed earlier, magicians plan what you will be thinking at every stage of the game, and we know the proper time to execute a secret move is when your attention is elsewhere.

In the theater, the most effective way to ultimately affect an audience is to have your performance build. If the peaks and valleys continue in a regular pattern—like a sine or cosine curve—then your audience will certainly feel that there is a rhythm to your presentation. This is a fine achievement. The audience rides with you up to the top and feels excitement, and then drops back down to their baseline while relaxing. Back up to the top with interest, and back down to the bottom with disinterest.

However, imagine if that sine curve was not horizontal but tilted upward diagonally, from left to right. Each mountain peak is successively higher than the one prior to it. Each valley is also higher than the previous valley. Now each moment of relaxation is not back at the baseline of disinterest but in a state of active arousal. By the time you reach the finale, the audience is in a heightened mind-set because their level of relaxation is also higher.

How can you, as a nonmagician, utilize this concept of peaks and valleys in business? The answer, again, is simple. Save the highlights of your speech, comment, or argument for the end so that you have somewhere to go. In the theater, actors learn that you should never begin a scene by shouting or screaming. It is difficult to build upon this level of intensity. Remember, if you can, Gene Wilder's terrific performance as Willy Wonka. He began as a calm and cool man but transformed into a compelling dynamo later in the movie.

Think of your own presentations in the same way, whether you are presenting to an audience of one or one thousand. Begin calmly and resist the urge to jump ahead to the point you want to make. This will take a degree of self-control. When all eyes are on you, it is common to want to shift attention away from yourself. Under pressure, many people blurt out what is most prevalent in their minds, and thus have nowhere to go in their argument or speech. I encourage you not to make this mistake. Instead, make your first point and then pull back. Make your next point with more enthusiasm, and then pull back again. Finally, make your last point—the most important one—once you've already cleared the first several peaks. I guarantee that the reaction to your presentation will be more effective than if you had tried jumping directly to the top.

WAIT A WEEK

I learned this concept of holding back so you have someplace to go by studying the career of magician Max Malini.

A master of human influence, Malini knew how to manipulate attention so that people would never catch him doing the "dirty work" (that's magic lingo for "secret moves"). Malini's *pièce de résistance* was the production of a solid block of ice from under a borrowed hat. It was a showstopper! While diverting the audience's attention elsewhere, he slipped the giant ice cube into the hat. And he never got caught. Here is one of Malini's great pieces of advice: Don't make the move when people are looking. If people continue to stare at your hands, just wait. How long should you wait? If necessary, he said, "wait a week." Be like a panther waiting to strike, and when the proper moment arises, pounce on it.

"Wait a week." A week! This is very profound advice, especially in this age of fast-paced movies and video games. People's attention spans become shorter every year. How is it possible to make people wait even a few extra seconds? Perhaps people were more forgiving in the first half of the twentieth century. Still, Malini sometimes waited so long that the ice cube melted entirely, until nothing was left to stick into the hat!

You can use Malini's advice in the real world too—outside of the magic arena. The idea of waiting a week means holding on to information until it is just the right time to present it. Of course, you don't have to take the "week" part of Malini's advice literally. The time you wait may be counted in minutes, hours, or months. Regardless of the length of time, the key is to wait for the proper moment. Do not rush forward with a piece of information or an action, despite your inclination to do so.

When you start a romantic relationship with someone, for instance, don't expect too much too soon. Wait to make the right move. Hold back from giving yourself away, to keep the other person on their toes. The other person will be delighted to see that you are not overly aggressive.

Lao-Tzu wrote: "Do you have the patience to wait until your mud settles and the water is clear? Can you remain unmoving until the right action arises on its own?"

The right moment will present itself. You do not need to force it. Malini waited as long as necessary to make his move. He didn't force people to look away. He let them do it in their own time. He apparently allowed others to command the situation, but really he was handing the reins over to them very briefly. You can do the same. Set up the framework and allow other people to navigate their way through that framework. You are in control because you set the boundaries, but you don't have to control *every aspect* of the situation. Let the other person take control of something seemingly inconsequential, while you control the main direction.

Remember: Malini knew that people would eventually look up.

BE AN AMBASSADOR

When people eventually look up and focus on you, do you know what they see? This final tip is more of a story than a secret. As you read it, however, it will hopefully act as a wake-up call that will help you reevaluate the way you present yourself to audiences. Here's the story.

On my last trip to San Francisco, I spent an afternoon with Joe Pon, the owner of Misdirections Magic Shop. There are dozens of magic shops all over the world where you can buy professional magician's props: feather flowers, gimmicked lacquer boxes, and tapered cards. In my travels, I've visited many such stores. But I really love Joe Pon's shop. It's a small, family-run shop that has hundreds of props, books, and instructional videos on the wall. A counter separates the front and the back of the store. And behind the counter sits a miniature Doberman pinscher named Vernon (named after the famous magician Dai Vernon). Joe trained his dog to protect the back of the store so that customers can't slip behind the counter and examine the props. As soon as you attempt to enter the rear area, Vernon's ears perk up. He scrunches his eyes and growls. If you take another step closer, he barks a ravenous bark to alert Joe that there is an intruder.

Joe really cares about magic, about secrets, and about the image magicians project to the public. He told me about a street performer who has worked Fisherman's Wharf for fifteen straight years. The performer—

a magician—has done his act thousands of times, and unfortunately, it shows. When he links and unlinks two solid steel rings, the magician acts completely disinterested. His eyes shift from side to side, and he pays no attention to his own trick. Despite the fact that he is performing an impossible act—*linking two solid rings*—he throws it away and focuses on hustling for tips.

Upset, Joe spoke to this street performer and reminded him of the importance of his role. "You are an *ambassador of magic*," urged Joe. "Thousands of tourists come to Fisherman's Wharf from all over the world. You may in fact be the first live magician that those people have ever seen in their lives. If you turn people off during your performance, they may carry that negative feeling for years to come."

The message is that there is no room for mediocrity. Remember: you are an ambassador for others in your group. If you are a rude salesperson, you are turning people off to dealing with your company. If you belong to a social organization or religious group, your attitude speaks far beyond your personal sphere. You are seen as part of a group, and unfortunately, you could become the launching pad for a negative stereotype against your group.

Event planners who have had a bad experience with a magician will not consider hiring a magician again. "Magic doesn't work," they say. But is that fair? Certainly there are other magicians who could do an excellent job. That one hack ruined their previous event shouldn't mean that "magic doesn't work." But that's not how people think.

The next time you introduce yourself and begin a personal interaction with others, remember how important your role is. You are the face of your company. You are the face of your organization. You are the face of your church. Other people will judge the larger organization based on their interactions with you.

GET TO WORK

The secrets in this chapter form the foundation of stronger and more dynamic presentations. Start applying them one at a time, and you will see a profound difference in the way that people receive the information that you present. From my experience, you'll probably have the most fun with Planned Failures.

I must warn you, though, that no matter how structurally sound your presentation, it'll fall flat if you have a dull personality. Audiences are captivated by charismatic individuals. The next chapter will introduce you to ways that you can develop your own charisma so that people will be fascinated by you even before you begin to speak.

TRUE TALES
FROM THE MILLIONAIRES' MAGICIAN

Anecdote 4
IMAGINARY VACATION

Comedian Michael Palin (of *Monty Python's Flying Circus*) and environmentalist David Bellamy sat in the radio studio with me. We were all guests on a prestigious British national talk show in London. When it was my turn to speak, the host challenged me to do magic on the radio! Sounds difficult, right? Here's what I did:

I asked David to think of his last vacation and to name the location aloud. He said, "Mauritius." I instructed him to imagine himself back in Mauritius—visualizing the sights, the smells, the sounds. He closed his eyes and played along. Then I startled him by snapping my fingers right in front of his nose.

"Right now, what are you imagining?"

"I was visualizing myself taking a walk on the beach," he said as he regained his focus.

"Good. A walk on the beach. All right, I need your help. I know this sounds crazy, but would you please take off your right shoe?"

He looked at me quizzically but agreed to play along some more. He handed me the shoe.

"A moment ago, you imagined yourself walking on the beach in Mauritius. Let's see how strong your imagination really is." The next moment, I tipped his shoe upside down and a long stream of *sand* poured out onto the table, forming a small pile. Michael Palin and the host were both beaming and uttering "Brilliant, brilliant" into their mics.

But I stopped them all and continued.

I said, "I didn't know that you were going to name Mauritius. But I could tell that you have a very vivid imagination. Please look inside your shoe. Is it empty?"

WIN THE CROWD   97

"Yes," said David.

"Please envision yourself back on the beach. In your mind's eye, picture that beach clearly. Good. Now reach inside your shoe again and tell us what you've found."

David reached into his own shoe and pulled out *a conch shell* that completely filled the interior. The crew inside the studio went wild, and the guests were completely flabbergasted.

Chapter Eight
CHARISMA

MEDIA MARKETERS RATE CELEBRITIES according to their Q-score, a number that measures a combination of visual appeal, believability, and warmth. The higher the Q-score, the more likeable that person is to a particular demographic group. Two factors contribute to the Q-score: the number of people who are aware of the celebrity, and the number of people who claim that celebrity as one of their favorites. But normal people like you and I don't number-crunch when we meet someone with charisma. We don't tabulate scores. We just *feel* something special about that person. We're drawn to him. We want to be near him, and we want to do business with him.

In this chapter, you'll learn the secret recipes for charisma that I've discovered as a magician. Many of these secrets I learned on the job, by watching my clients interact with their guests at society gatherings. Although I'm hired as an entertainer, I've also acted as a student of human nature. I count myself lucky to have had the chance to see many of New York's top movers and shakers in action. I've seen how they make an entrance, work the room, and leave people talking. Several patterns emerged as I observed them, and I incorporated those patterns into my performances.

You can do the same. Charisma is not something you are born with, it's something you develop. And it's certainly worth developing. Beyond just public speaking, charisma is often a deal-sealer and attracts people to you.

Here are what I feel are the qualities that make up a charismatic person. We'll look at each of them in turn.

Charismatic people are

- **enthusiastic,**
- **confident,**
- **comfortable in their own skin,**
- **unconcerned about what others think of them,**
- **masters of their subject matter, and**
- **symbols of something others desire.**

STEPS TO BECOMING CHARISMATIC

Be Enthusiastic

A lively presenter can resuscitate even the deadest audience. When you begin speaking—either socially or professionally—remember that listeners model their responses on *your* behavior. They're waiting for you to motivate them. Most people are starving for worthwhile stimulation. Be enthusiastic, and they'll sense that you are telling them something important.

My high school physics teacher was so enthusiastic about his subject that even students with little interest in science were enraptured. Students from other classes complained that physics was their least favorite subject, while my classmates and I couldn't wait for his next class. It's clearly not the material that made my teacher's lessons more compelling. He had the same curriculum as every other physics teacher. What made the difference was his genuine passion and enthusiasm for the topic.

Even if you've said your lines a hundred times, act as if it's the first time. It's easy to get into a rut and deliver your lines like you always do. The moment that you slip into automatic pilot, you lose genuine enthusiasm. Audiences can sense when something is fresh or when it is canned.

> An artist is a person who always sees the world in a new way, as if for the
> first time, and is able to make it possible for others as well.
> —*René Schickelé*

Don't rest on your laurels just because you've given the same presentation, sales pitch, or class more than a few times. Instead, use your comfort with the material as leverage. Focus on the delivery, not the content. You are freer to play with the delivery because you already know the content so well. Recall the first time you spoke those words and feel enthusiastic about them yourself. You won't be acting or pretending. It'll be genuine. That's when people will be drawn to you, and to what you have to say.

Show Confidence

Audiences can sense when you're scared or self-conscious. Show them any indication that you're insecure and they'll lose interest fast.

People are naturally drawn to those who show confidence. Notice I said *show* confidence, not simply *be* confident. It doesn't do much good if you are confident while standing quietly in the corner. Charismatic people show audiences their confidence by the way they stand, the way they speak, and the things they say. Chapter 4, "Building Confidence Before the Curtain Rises," introduced many techniques that you can implement immediately to demonstrate your own confidence. Remember the staring contest and the movie theater exercises? Go back and reread these, and actually try them if you haven't already.

Feel Comfortable in Your Own Skin

Charisma lies deeper than your physical appearance. It's in your spirit. People are drawn to others who are comfortable in their own skin. Are you dissatisfied with your looks? Get over it. That's not what audiences truly care about. Comedian Jimmy Durante was born with a gigantic nose—his "schnozz"—that could've repulsed people by its grotesque size. But instead of detracting from his personality, it enhanced his character. He was proud of his looks, poking his nose high into the air after each performance. Durante became one of America's most beloved entertainers of the 1940s.

If people sense that you're trying too hard to impress them, your behavior actually acts like a red flag. It makes them wonder whether you're trying to hide or overcompensate for something. In *Hamlet*, Shakespeare writes, "The lady doth protest too much." The phrase "doth protest too much" means to insist so passionately that something is true that people suspect the exact opposite. Beginning magicians get caught in this trap all the time. They say, "Here I have a perfectly ordinary pack of cards." However, the audience thinks, "Why is he making such an issue about the pack being perfectly ordinary? I'll bet that there's actually something fishy."

Be proud of who you are. Be proud of your heritage, your accent, your family, and your looks. You are a unique individual, and others are attracted to what makes you unique. The more comfortable you are with yourself, the more attractive you are to others.

Be Unconcerned About What Others Think of You

The key to charisma may lie in this advice. Do what seems right to you, and don't waver when people present differing points of view. Stay true to who you are and what you believe in. People will often test you to see how far you can be pushed. Don't budge. The firmer you stand, the clearer it is what you stand for.

At social and business gatherings, ask questions that no one else would ask. Don't worry if you think people will find you foolish. The odds are high that others were thinking the same questions but were too self-conscious to ask. Those people will be drawn to you for your courage to speak aloud what they kept locked inside. Leaders are able to voice the thoughts that their followers wish they could clearly express.

Not everybody will like you, and that's perfectly okay. There is no need to be liked by every person you meet. People will dislike you for the oddest reasons. They may dislike your clothes, your attitude, your company, your name, or your breath. You may remind them of someone they disliked in junior high school. Or they may be prejudiced against your race or religion. Face it, you can't please everybody. There's no need to expect that you can. No matter how hard you try, there will always be someone who isn't bowled over by your charm. If that's the case, why exert yourself trying to achieve an unattainable goal?

Stop trying to impress everyone. Your presentations will improve, and people will be more attracted to you when you decide to impress no one but yourself.

Be the Master of Your Subject Matter

Be so good they can't ignore you.
—*Jerry Dunn*

Audiences will always applaud skill. A display of skill confirms to onlookers that you're capable of delivering the goods. Think of how impressed people are when they witness an Olympic gymnast giving a masterful performance. Spectators feel something special about that athlete because they can imagine how hard she must have trained. Upon witnessing greatness, people often feel inspired. They're reminded that human potential is limitless.

Just be sure to keep your ego in check. Never show off simply to make yourself look good. Nothing turns off an audience more quickly than a hotshot. If you have skill, there's no need to flaunt it.

Instead, follow the Japanese proverb "The clever hawk hides its claws." Be understated about your abilities. Reveal your skill only when appropriate. People will be more impressed when they discover what you're capable of on their own. They'll wonder what other secret abilities you possess, and they'll want to get to know more about you. Give them a sense of what you're capable of, and they'll be hungry for more. Your reputation consists of a combination of observable and imagined traits.

There is certainly a time and place for demonstrating skill. When you're giving a presentation, for instance, it helps to reveal your skill early on, simply to establish your credentials. I perform three difficult card manipulations near the start of my show, to let people know that they're in good hands. But then I back off. No more overt displays of skill for the rest of the show. My philosophy is to introduce the skill, then retreat. Less is always more. There's no need to overprove. In general, people will be more impressed by your skill when they see that you're humble about it. If you do something extraordinarily well and then shrug it off as nothing special, audiences are relieved by your humility.

Be a Symbol of Something Others Desire

You've probably had several role models throughout your life. You were attracted to them because of certain well-defined qualities they possessed. You looked to your role models for guidance or advice because they personified qualities that you yourself lacked. You strove to reach a higher level by emulating those people.

We are often drawn to people who have things that we wish for ourselves, such as health, success, power, strong morals, discipline, energy, and drive. If you possess qualities like these, people will want to be around you. They hope that by being near you, they will be able to improve their own lives.

CONTROL YOURSELF TO THE TOP

I just divided charisma into six steps for you, but that's not the only way to achieve it. Another way I like to explain charisma to people is through the vantage point of control.

There are four major areas that you must learn to control: time, space, language, and appearance.

Control of Time

Most people rush when they speak. I know that I did. When I was growing up, I used to hurry through my performances with hopes that a quick delivery would hold the audience's attention. My friend Mark Sicher taught me to slow down. Mark was studying cello at the prestigious LaGuardia High School for Music and Art and Performing Arts. One day while practicing, his teacher told him that he was playing too quickly. The teacher said, "If you play so that it feels slow to *you*, it will be just right for the audience." Why is this true?

People can only accept a certain amount of new information each minute. If you overload them, they'll only take in a small amount. For you it's old; for them it's new. In search of something novel, your mind glosses over the stuff you already know, so you move quickly through the information that you are familiar with. Other people, however, are being exposed to your ideas for the first time. Their brains need extra time to process the new stimulation. The key here is to speak and move slower than you normally do. Give other people time to let your information sink in.

Another benefit to speaking and moving slowly is that you will appear more self-assured. The successful people I've observed take their time. They give weight to their words. Try doing this yourself. When you take your time, people will believe that you must be saying something important. They will feel that you are worth giving their time to. When you talk more slowly, people will wait for you, and then you can control the pace of your encounter with them.

Have the mind-set of an artist: follow your own vision and make people conform to you, instead of the other way around. I've been hired to entertain at parties with revved-up dance music, which is far from my style of performing. On these occasions, there was no way that I could have been effective if I'd tried to speed my pace up to that of the Latin dance music. Instead, I brought the audience to my pace. I slowed down. You have to know what your pace is and how you work most effectively.

Remember: he who keeps the other person waiting is in control. No doubt you've experienced this at the doctor's office or a job interview. The person who causes the wait builds anticipation about the meeting within the mind of the person kept waiting. That's why I always begin my shows later than the announced time. On Broadway they do this too. Producers start the shows ten minutes late because they want to build anticipation.

When you make people wait, you have the upper hand. People become hungry for your pacing. If you examine the behavior of people who work for a billionaire, for example, they usually act very rapidly—like worker bees serving the queen bee. The queen stays in the hive while the workers flit here and there. The billionaire watches his staff move quickly while he stands firm and expects results. He doesn't need to move quickly, because he has other people who will do this for him.

Control of Space

I have a strange habit. When I am seated at a restaurant, I rearrange the salt shakers, dishes, and flower vases that are on the tabletop. Anything that is blocking or taking up space in front of me has got to move. When I first started this habit, I consciously did it so that I had an unimpeded view of the people across the table from me. That's practical, right? If the flowers are blocking you from seeing other people's faces, it makes sense to shove them off to the side.

But there's another benefit to this habit. By staking claim to a larger space, you expand your personal boundaries beyond yourself. You become a landlord for the space around you. Remember, people respect others who control large plots of real estate. It's pretty clear that some of the grandest mansions and estates are owned by people who have succeeded in their chosen fields. You can do the same, even at the restaurant table. By staking out your own area, you will appear larger than life, because you are not blending in with your environment. Instead, you are making the space conform to you.

If you expand your personal boundaries, you can make yourself more charismatic as well. There are many ways to do this—at social gatherings, in the office, or at meetings. Here's one technique you can try at your next meeting. When you sit down, place a pile of books in front of you. They could be notebooks, legal pads, or any other bulky books. The books should block you partially from view. In other words, the people you are meeting with will only be able to see part of your body. Your section of the table will look cluttered. However, when it is your turn to speak, abruptly shove all of the books off to the side, clearing a large space in front of yourself. The sudden contrast between your being "blocked off" and now "wide open" serves as a surprise to others. You have provided them with new information—something that they did not see before. Are they going to pay attention? You bet. You've molded the space to suit your needs. You've acted on a strategy that is based on how the mind works. Other people have no choice but to perk up their ears because their eyes have alerted them that you are worth listening to.

Another way of increasing your personal space is to become taller. Our society is influenced by tall people. I believe that this stems from our childhood experiences. Think back to when you were a child. Since you were small, you looked up at your parents and teachers. You looked up to authority. Because of your size, you had no choice. All of the bigger people made the rules, and you had to follow them. They held authority based on their relative position. It makes sense that this carries over into our adult lives. We "look up to" people we respect.

So how can you become taller? One technique is to wear platform shoes—shoes with thicker soles and high heels. I learned this secret from

mentalist Max Maven, who claims to have influenced some very prestigious names in show business to wear platform shoes. (In Japanese, by
the way, they are called "secret boots." Isn't that hysterical?) Such shoes
make you appear taller, more commanding, and they force you to walk
more gracefully. We often assume that high heels are only for women, but
even men can wear shoes with thicker soles. To see what I mean, try on a
pair of cowboy boots and take a stroll around the shoe store. Each step you
take will be much more deliberate. You will feel like John Wayne. It may
be awkward at first, but once you have the hang of it, you will be taller and
more graceful.

If you aren't thrilled with the idea of wearing platform shoes, you will
love this next secret. There is a technique to help people "grow" and feel
more confident that I learned many years ago from a chiropractor. Try
this right now. Stand up and walk to the nearest wall. Stand so that your
heels, shoulders, and the back of your head touch the wall. It helps to tuck
your chin in slightly. Wriggle your body until you really sink into the wall
and you feel yourself elongate upward. Remember to keep your shoulders
against the wall; don't hunch them or your head forward. Once you've gotten yourself in position, take one step away from the wall. It is important
that you keep your body in alignment. Do not let your posture fade. You
should feel proud and strong. Take a deep breath. Believe it or not, you
probably just grew about an inch and a half.

I taught this technique to a very short man who was the director of a financial company in New York (he is only five feet four). He used to feel
self-conscious about his height. After correcting his own posture every
day, however, he told me that he felt taller, and that others thought more
highly of him. In fact, I spoke to one of his colleagues who told me that
now *he* is the one looking down upon others. He learned to tilt his head in
such a way that he peers down his nose at people and appears to be very
much their equal, despite his God-given height.

It is not that difficult to alter the way that you present yourself. By
making a few adjustments in the way you control space, you change the
way that others view you. I learned this from watching Gene Anderson, a
successful magician and retired executive at Dow Chemical. When Gene

talks with you one-on-one, he gives you his full attention. He does this by moving close—very close—so *his* face is right in *your* face. He fills your entire field of vision with his lively eyes and warm smile. It seems as if you are the world to him. There is no room for distractions or roaming eyes. Talk about making a connection! As a result, people adore Gene. (Don't forget to pop a breath mint before trying this.)

In fact, there is a proven psychological principle at work here. When you are closer to something, you have an increased desire to attain it. At a soccer match, for instance, the people closer to the front door of the stadium push harder than those at the back, because they are *almost* inside. Their desire to enter becomes greater because they are closer. This finding holds true across the board. Watch yourself when you drive. See how you speed up once you're near your exit? The proximity to your goal makes your desire to achieve it greater.

You can use this principle to change the experience of your meetings and personal interactions. In addition to standing closer to people, you can also control the layout of the room. I have experimented with the layout of chairs and furniture at my show *Chamber Magic*. The closer I stand to the audience, the greater the impact they feel. When I tried performing at events where a large dance floor stood between the stage riser and the front row, it was difficult to connect with the audience. But when I shifted the riser closer to the front row of audience members, they treated me like a king. Same show, different experience.

Control of Language

I'm certain that you have had days where everything you said came out just right. The words you wanted to say flowed effortlessly from your lips, and your vocabulary was right on the money. People paid attention to you and laughed at your observations. Well, guess what—you can learn to be "on" like this every day.

Like many entertainers, I keep files of jokes and anecdotes that I can refer to when looking for the perfect thing to say. When you hear a comedian ad-lib, the odds are that he is hardly ad-libbing at all. Instead, he is likely saying something he's said in the past and stored in his mental file. When the opportunity arises, he pulls the perfect saying out of "nowhere" and everyone falls on the floor laughing.

You can do something very similar. However, there is no need to write down jokes. Instead, I suggest that you write down single words and brief phrases. That's right. Just like when you were studying for the SAT exams. I'll explain how you should do this in just a moment. But first let's look at why this is effective.

Many of the successful people I have met use precise language. They say what they mean, using just the right words to do so. Instead of showing off their fancy vocabulary, they use technical words to articulate their thoughts when the situation calls for it. There is no need to be lexiphanic—someone who uses impressive words for effect. (Oops—I couldn't resist!)

As a magician, I've learned that what I say is as important as what I do. You can influence people's thoughts by the words you use when you speak. One way to become a better speaker is to find an author that you like and try to incorporate his vivid words into your language. Also, read the *New York Times* to stay current, and understand the language used in technology, culture, and business. Customize your vocabulary so that you don't sound like everyone else. I do this by keeping a word book.

To do this, first buy a pocket-sized notepad. (It's important that you carry your word book with you at all times.) Anytime you find an unusual word or phrase, write it down. Perhaps you like the sound or the look of the word. Or maybe you like the thing that the word represents. It might evoke some pleasant associations in your mind. Whatever the reason, write it down in your word book. When you are waiting in a doctor's office or at a traffic light, flip through the pages and review the words that you've selected to remember. Then, challenge yourself to use the words in your daily life. Try not to sound awkward. The proper moment will arise. Remember the comedian who "ad-libs"? You will master the words through usage, so stay alert and see how soon you can incorporate them into your conversations.

I used this technique extensively when I was studying Japanese as a foreign language. On the left side of the page, I wrote the new word that I wanted to learn. On the right side, I used that word in a sentence. Since *you* select the words yourself, you will likely remember the context in which they were first used when you heard them. This is much more effective than if someone were to hand you a list of random vocabulary words to memorize. Page through your customized word book throughout the day so that the words are fresh in your mind. Studies show that you "own" a word after using it three times in real conversation. Challenge yourself to do this, and you will become a more interesting and articulate speaker.

Another skill to master is to eliminate filler sounds and words. These are words like "umm," "uh," "like," and "y'know." They make you sound noncommittal, as if you don't know what you are talking about. If you use such words too often, people may wonder why they're even listening to you. Try recording yourself and listen to how often you are guilty of using filler words. Use a tape recorder to record your next telephone call; you may be unpleasantly surprised. The key is to increase the precision of your speech. Anytime you feel yourself about to say "umm," just be silent. Make people wait for you. You've heard the expression "hanging on every word," right? You can make your audiences hang on your every word by pausing when you would normally say a filler word. As you search for the next thing to say, people will believe you are giving deep thought to your ideas. Little will they know that you are making a conscious effort to reduce your "umms"! The more you are aware of your tendency to use filler words, the sooner you will be able to eliminate them entirely from your speech.

As you build your vocabulary and learn how to get people going with your precise and unique style of speaking, you may find yourself becoming the center of attention more often. You will need to make sure that others can hear you, so don't be shy. Speak up. As an entertainer, I learned how to raise the volume of my voice. Onstage, I aim to be a little larger than life. If you speak too softly, people will have to strain. However, if you speak slightly louder than is necessary, others will turn to hear you. And then they will wonder why everyone else is listening to you. Curiosity will get the best of them, and suddenly they will be wrapped up in your talk too. The only exception to this is when you are speaking to just one person. Obviously there is no need to be over the top and loud in this case. In fact, when I am talking to one person alone, I usually lower my voice so that the person is forced to move in closer and pay attention.

Control of Appearance

One of the most difficult challenges I face as a magician is to step back and see myself as others see me. For example, it is easy to delude myself into thinking that my sleight of hand is fooling people when it's really not. This happens when I focus on what *I* think about myself, versus the experience of others who are watching. There is a mental leap a professional magician has to take to be able to see things through the eyes of the audience. This shift in thinking applies not only to tricky moves but to appearance too. Do you know how *you* appear to others?

I believe that anything you *can* control, you *should* control. Look down at your feet right now. Are you wearing scuffed shoes? No one made you put them on today. Everything you wear is the result of a conscious choice. If you have two pairs of shoes—one looks good and the other is scuffed—toss the scuffed ones. People do notice. Remember when you were a kid and wore new shoes? What did the other kids say as soon as you walked into school? "New shoes!" (And then they probably stepped on your toes . . .) This attention to detail carries over to our adult life. It's been said that a woman looks at a man in three places: his eyes, his watch, and his shoes. Tend to the details in your appearance, as they will not go unnoticed. Oh yes, get a nice haircut too.

I'm fortunate that my clients have invited me many times to perform in such private clubs as the Metropolitan Club in New York and the Boca Raton Resort and Club in Florida. The members of these exclusive clubs dress in a way that helps them exude power. They wear rich fabrics, subtle patterns, and distinctive accessories. I remember what type of clothing they wear and make a mental note to hunt down similar clothes for my-self. By exposing yourself to style, you learn about being stylish. It's not innate—you have to spend time learning to recognize good fashion sense.

In order to build your knowledge, go into an expensive store that sells the highest-end clothing in your area. It could be Barney's, Neiman Marcus, or Saks Fifth Avenue. Walk around the store and touch the clothes. Feel the fabric. In the garment business, they call fabric texture the "hand." Find fabrics that have a good hand. Don't be shy about trying on the most expensive suits or dresses in the store. Remember Maxim 1: Be Bold. Learn what it feels like to envelop yourself in luxury. If you find one item that makes you look and feel great, it may be worth the investment.

While you are clothes shopping, look at the other customers. People often get dressed up in their best clothes to go shopping, especially in high-end stores. Fortunately, you can learn from them by looking at their choices. What they're wearing can become an example for you. If you're afraid of being caught staring, then take a look at what the mannequins are wearing! I'm serious. Usually, professional stylists dress the man-nequins. Rather than try to find things that match on your own, look at the stylists' choices. You can find similar, knock-off items at lower-priced stores. These stores copy the higher-end stores within the same season, so you can still look stylish without having to spend exorbitantly.

If you can afford it, though, have your clothes tailor-made. There's nothing wrong with buying your clothes off the rack (or off the "peg," as they say in England). But the extra expense is justified. Custom-tailored clothes form perfectly to your body. For this reason, they won't wear down in the wrong places.

Also, you may want to consider buying some sort of eye-catcher, something that is unique to you. It could be a butterfly pendant or an in-teresting pair of glasses that you always wear. Entertainers often find a unique look and then capitalize on it for years. You can do the same. Find something that people will identify with you. My lovely client Violy McCausland wears long, flowing shoulder wraps that have become a part of her signature look. Aldon James, president of the National Arts Club in Gramercy Park, wears a hand-tied bow tie, and a pen with a squiggly metal clip that perches out from his breast pocket. Each of these eye-catchers helps to define the character of the person. If a stranger had to pick you up from the train station, which would be the easier way to describe yourself: "I'm wearing a blue overcoat and khaki pants" or "I'm wearing a gray fedora with a red and yellow feather"?

CHARISMA IS one of the most mysterious of all human traits. Study people who you consider to be charismatic. Observe how they talk, how they act, and how they move. If someone has a particular trait that you admire, emulate it in your own way. Don't copy it. Instead, modify it until it becomes a part of you. Herman Melville wrote, "It's better to fail in originality than succeed in imitation." Strive to be original. Your charisma depends on it.

TRUE TALES
FROM THE MILLIONAIRES' MAGICIAN

Anecdote 5
GET SMART

When I received a telephone call from astronomer Carl Sagan, I thought it was a prank. My college friends and I used to pull pranks on one another constantly. For instance, we once fiddled with the circuits on a math major's calculator the night before a test. Every time he pressed a key, the wrong number showed up on the screen.

So I was sure that the voice on the other end of the line was one of my friends, not Dr. Sagan himself. The voice said, "I've heard wonderful things about your close-up magic. Would you be willing to give a demonstration for me?" I almost said something sarcastic, but then remembered that one of my professors had promised to introduce me to Sagan before I graduated. And no matter how good my friends were, none of them could imitate the astronomer's distinctive baritone. Sure enough, it was really him.

Dr. Sagan explained that he would be hosting a group of visiting astrophysicists, and he wanted me to give a talk about the psychology that makes magic work (much of which I've presented in this book). After my talk, he wanted me to present my magic and mind-reading show. I hesitated to accept the invitation. How could I possibly baffle some of the smartest people alive? If anyone could catch me out, *this* would be the group. Sagan assured me that everything would be just fine.

I arrived at Cornell University's Space Sciences Building and presented my talk and show. As amazed as the scientists were, I was even more amazed myself when they gave me a standing ovation. It was one of the highlights of my career.

Ever since, I've told people that if they don't understand how I do what I do, they're in very good company. Some of the smartest people in the world have no idea either.

Chapter Nine
READING PEOPLE

CHARISMATIC INDIVIDUALS USE THEIR personal charm to influence crowds of people. But charm is a one-way street. You can only demonstrate your wares so much before people tire of them. I believe that the truly charismatic person has the ability to turn the tables and focus on other people.

Knowing how to read an audience is an essential skill for every magician. Each audience is different, and the group dynamic within that audience changes every night. I read the audience in order to respond to them. This helps make each presentation more effective. Let me teach you some of what I've learned.

Here is a drill that will strengthen your power of observation. This is essential when you attempt to read your audiences.

A HUNDRED STEPS IN DARKNESS

Go to a park or other open space where you can walk a hundred steps straight ahead without bumping into anything. You're going to be walking with your eyes closed. Don't worry, you'll be breaking this down in groups of ten steps, so it's not as dangerous as it sounds.

Close your eyes and walk forward ten steps, counting each step silently as you take it. When you reach ten, open your eyes for a moment and remember as much of your surroundings as you can. Then close your eyes and take ten more steps.

Start thinking of your eyes as a camera's shutter and open them only for a split second. Every tenth step, open your eyes and force yourself to remember everything in front of you. Is there a small ditch, a curve in the path, a small animal? Once you've closed your eyes again, trust your memory. Repeat the ten steps ten times. Don't break the rhythm of your walk.

At first you will feel wobbly and insecure. It's not easy to balance and keep a rhythmic step with your eyes closed. Don't worry. You only have to take one hundred steps. You'll get better each time you practice.

At the end of each ten paces your brain will be starving for visual stimulation. The shutter-view floods your brain with information. You will see small details that you never recognized before. You'll become more aware of items normally only captured by your peripheral vision—on the extreme sides. You'll see more than you've ever seen before. It's like watching a letterbox edition of a movie on a high-definition television. Colors will appear more vibrant, and the details of your surroundings will etch themselves into your memory. Your survival relies on it.

You may think that only a lunatic would walk through the park with his eyes closed. Guess again! Compared to what I'm about to suggest, walking through the park blind will seem like, well, a walk in the park.

Once you've gained confidence with this drill in a relatively safe location, try it on a crowded city street. I've even practiced this in New York's Grand Central Station. Amid all the hustle and bustle, your split-second glances will force you to remember much more than in the park. You'll learn to anticipate the movements of people, and you'll remember your relative distance to them. After practicing A Hundred Steps in Darkness for many years, I know just when to stop so that I don't bump into people, dogs, or baby carriages.

What have you learned from this drill? You've sharpened your skills of observation. You've learned to take in more information at a single glance. You are now ready to read people before they are even aware that you've begun.

Characters in Sir Arthur Conan Doyle's stories sometimes assumed that the mysterious detective was a mind reader. However, as Sherlock Holmes explained to his sidekick, Dr. Watson, he was not psychic at all. He was just more observant than most.

You can be too. Apply your new awareness to every person you meet, capturing as many physical details as you can in a glance. It'll make people feel uncomfortable if you shift your eyes up and down, so be subtle about it. Trust your greater awareness.

First, I always look at people's hands, because hands tell you a lot about the person connected to them. In our culture we shake hands when first meeting. That's a good excuse to look down momentarily. Quickly note any jewelry, such as rings, watches, cuff links, and bracelets. I always try to glimpse any words that are indicated on the jewelry: a school name written on the side of a class ring, a company name on the face of a watch, or the person's name hanging from a bracelet pendant. This gives you additional information about the person and puts you in a position of power. You can now move from general to specific very quickly by extrapolating a profile of the type of person who would go to that school, or work at that company.

As you shake the person's hand, also take note of his skin texture. Is it coarse or smooth? Calloused or supple? This distinction helps you figure out his occupation. Rough hands suggest a laborer: a carpenter, plumber, or shopkeeper. Soft, silky hands suggest an office worker or a professional (doctor, attorney, architect, financier). If you meet an office worker who uncharacteristically has rough hands, you can infer that he has a weekend hobby that gets him outdoors: camping, fishing, or golfing. Without speaking a word or asking a question, you know something about his life outside of the office.

Why would you want to do this? You will be able to create stronger rapport when you focus on what you have in common with others. The detailed clues you discover may reveal a topic of conversation that you wouldn't have otherwise thought to explore.

As a magician, I look for these details so that I can surprise people. If I glimpse a company name on a watch, IBM, for instance, I may pretend to read the person's mind by feeding that information back to him in bits and pieces. "I'm sensing that you are a very analytical person. You thrive in structured environments. Does Armonk, New York, mean anything to you? I'm getting a name. Sam Palm. I'm not sure who that is." The man I've just met will flip out because I've named the town of IBM's corporate headquarters (which I happen to know is Armonk), and an abbreviation of his CEO's name: Samuel Palmisano (which I know because I read the *Wall Street Journal*). Everyone watching is surprised, and they credit me with psychic abilities.

You have no need to pretend you're psychic. So here's how you can use the information you've learned. It's simple. Mention what you've noticed out loud. Be obvious about it. Use the information to build rapport. If you glimpse the IBM logo on someone's watch, say, "Oh, do you work at IBM? I saw your watch. I'm involved in online commerce myself. What division do you work in?" And away you go. You've latched onto something that you observed and used it as a hook to start a conversation that will bring the two of you closer together.

Here's a sneaky trick that I've used to gain even more information about people. It may be too audacious for you. Remember, magicians are opportunists, and we act boldly to stay a few steps ahead of our audiences. That's Maxim 1: Be Bold. When you see someone's handbag open on the floor, contrive a way to glimpse inside it. One way is to "accidentally" drop something (a pen, paper clip, etc.) to the floor. While you're bending down to pick it up, peek inside the open bag and see if there are any documents, receipts, postcards, or other items visible. Any information you acquire will tell you just a little bit more about the person.

I'm not advocating that you stick your hand inside the person's bag and shuffle through their things! No. I believe in respecting people's property. My training as a magician, though, has taught me to jump on these kinds of opportunities to impress the person I'm speaking with. Remember the first Maxim of Magic: Be Bold.

THINKING ABOUT WHAT THEY'RE THINKING ABOUT

Living in Japan taught me a lesson about mind reading. As a culture, the Japanese read the minds of others on a daily basis. They are sensitive to others' thoughts and feelings. Before taking any action that involves someone else, they think about how that person will perceive their action. They take considerable time to discuss how other people are likely to react. They don't want to embarrass others or make them "lose face." Put simply, *they think about what the other person is thinking about*.

It seemed so effortless to my Japanese colleagues. They reeled off the multiple outcomes without even blinking. "If we do this, then he'll think this way. But if we do that, then he'll think that way." Since I didn't grow up in Japan, I had to train myself to improve this skill. Here's how you do it.

Whenever you're waiting by yourself—at the post office, the checkout counter, a restaurant—find one person who is far away from you and start watching him. (When you get better at this, you can practice with people who are standing closer to you. For now, begin with someone who's far away.) Imagine what is going through that person's mind. Pay attention to what he is looking at and imagine how you would respond if you were in his place. Picture yourself in his situation. Really see yourself there. You are training to think like another person. There's no pressure on either of you, since he is located far away. If he moves out of view, the game's over. Just start with someone new.

The more you practice, the more you'll be able to predict the other person's behavior. You will, literally, be able to read his mind. Once I was in New York's Central Park and I was observing a young man who was rollerblading. At full speed, he lost balance and wiped out. He got up, looked around, and brushed himself off as if nothing had happened. He acted cool, since he knew other people had seen him fall. He skated away as if nothing had happened. I leaned over to my friend and said, "Watch this. He's going to sit down on that bench over there." Sure enough, the skater stopped, looked at the bench, and sat down. He rubbed his bruises and slouched his body, obviously in a great deal of pain.

How'd I do it? I put myself into his shoes (skates, actually). If *I* had wiped out in front of other people, I'd probably think, "I hope none of these people know me. They'll tell this story to my friends. How embarrassing." I'd get away from the spotlight, the area of interest where everyone was paying attention. And then I'd want to evaluate my injury in private. That's exactly what went through the skater's head.

When you start to observe people regularly, you learn how to empathize with them. And you'll see how your own emotions often overlap with the behavior that you observe. As you learned earlier in this book, Max Malini knew that people behave in predictable ways, given certain circumstances. Although we all believe that we are unique, we share the fact that we are humans. The most personal experience is the most universal. Think of how you would react in a given situation; it is highly likely that others would respond similarly.

UNCONSCIOUS VISIBLE RESPONSES

Once you've started achieving success in predicting people's behavior from afar, try the same exercise with people more close by. Because you're nearer, you have the advantage of seeing minute physiological changes in their faces. Genie LaBorde got it right in her book *Influencing with Integrity* when she defined these changes as "unconscious visible responses." People aren't aware that they are giving off these signals, but you'll be able to read them. In poker, they're called "tells," since the signals tell other players what type of hand you're holding. The ability to read such tells is extremely helpful in learning whether someone is lying or telling the truth, which you'll learn how to do later in this chapter.

When you speak with people, notice subtle changes in their

- **skin color,**
- **facial muscles and lower lip, and**
- **breathing.**

Don't fret if it sounds difficult to observe these characteristics *at all*, let alone changes in them. When you start paying attention you'll learn to recognize even the most minute changes. These changes serve as road signs to the person's inner state. In this section you'll learn how to recognize subtle physiological variations and use them to determine what people are thinking.

You may believe this is an impossible claim. How can someone's skin color tell you what she's thinking? I confess that there is no absolute relationship. If a person's face flushes in a certain way, this doesn't automatically indicate that she's thinking about a trip to Bermuda. Not at all. Your observations are merely that—observed responses. However, these responses help you calibrate the person's thought processes. Before I start a card trick, I spend time showing people red cards, and then black cards. As I'm talking, I flash a handful of same colored cards to specific people, and I see how they respond. There's no rush, and I do this as I'm casually talking.

After twenty seconds, I've zeroed in on the audience's responses to reds versus blacks. I know, for instance, that a lady in the second aisle tightens her bottom lip when she sees red cards, but relaxes the muscles around her mouth when she sees black cards. When I begin performing a trick, I approach that woman and ask her to remove any card at random. I ask her to look at her selection and think of whether it's red or black. I observe her jaw and lip and evaluate whether she's taken a red or black card.

I should mention that I calibrate more than just reds and blacks. Through practice, I've learned to distinguish responses based on suit (clubs, hearts, spades, diamonds) and value (ace through king). Sometimes I put the deck of cards away and ask a participant to merely think of a card. By observing her face, I can work out what card she is likely thinking of.

Yes, there is certainly room for error. I only choose people to participate in my performances, however, if I think they will be cooperative. I find the people who respond most readily to my suggestions, and then ask them to step forward. It appears as if I've chosen someone "at random," but in fact I've chosen someone who will help bring the demonstration to a successful conclusion. I have successfully built rapport with that person and he genuinely wants me to succeed.

You have it much easier. Most of the time, you interact with people you already know. You have a head start because you know the ways they tend to think. Here are some tools that will help you dig deeper so you'll be able to anticipate their responses before they open their mouths.

Your Three-Day Exercise

Not all people respond in the same way. There is no specific formula that you can follow. That's why I'm going to present you with several different behaviors to observe. If you're not able to assess any feedback in one behavior, look for the next. Go down the list until you succeed with one. The best way I've learned to practice observing these is to focus on one per day.

Skin Color

On Day 1, devote yourself to watching for changes in people's skin color. Faces change color and hue on a moment-to-moment basis. If you've never paid attention to this before, you're in for a surprise. Try to pick out each color that you see on people's faces. You may find shades of pink, brown, blue, purple, orange, yellow, and gray. Skin is not one uniform color but an amalgam of many. These colors appear brighter or duller depending on the person's mood, thoughts, and emotional state.

Your drill today is to observe, and then influence, the contrasting colors on three different people's faces. Try this drill with three friends or coworkers. With each person, pay attention to the resting tones of his face before you provide any stimulation. Now say something embarrassing to him. Remind him of a mistake he made in the past or chastise him for a recent error. You'll see him blush. Look carefully at the change in skin tone, and also note where on his face those changes occur. Some people blush in splotchy areas of their cheeks, while others sport an overall redness.

Next, say something that eases his painful memory. Tell a joke or lighthearted story. Watch how his facial coloration changes again. In my experience, I've found that the tip of the nose turns red when people recall a happy memory, but remains unchanged when they are embarrassed. The degree of this coloration shift varies from person to person.

You may feel the urge to stare intently at your friends' faces. When you are just starting out this is acceptable. As you improve, though, you won't have to stare as hard to distinguish these indicators.

Later in this chapter, you'll learn how to apply this information to read people's thoughts and feelings. But first, let's look at some more indicators.

Facial Muscles and Lower Lip

On Day 2, shift your attention to the minute changes in your friends' facial muscles. Observe such changes near the jawbone when they clench their teeth together. Pay attention to their nostrils too. Many people flare their nostrils when they are upset over something. They also raise or lower their eyebrows, crinkling their forehead and the folds between their eyes.

During the course of conversation, ask your three friends to talk about something that disturbed them recently—a speeding ticket, a lawsuit, or some other upsetting episode. Watch how their faces build and release tension in different areas, and remember these patterns for each person.

Also direct your attention to the lower lip. It is not possible to consciously control the lower lip, so this feature is a true indicator of the person's inner state. You'll notice that the lower lip trembles slightly right before a person begins speaking. And then it changes shape, color, and size depending on the person's mood. Remember the different patterns of each person's lower lip, and associate each pattern with the emotions that he is demonstrating. Store them as mental photographs. Later on, when you observe the same lip pattern, match it with your mental photograph and you'll know what he is thinking before he even speaks.

Breathing

On Day 3, challenge yourself to note the breathing patterns of your three friends. I say "challenge" because sometimes it is difficult to notice people's breathing. Neckties, vests, and tight clothing may prevent you from seeing the up-and-down rhythm of people's chests. That's okay. Watch their shoulders and necks. There's one thing you know for sure: they *are* breathing. So fine-tune your observations and pick out the rhythms as best you can.

More important, note when those rhythms *change*. Any alteration in a person's breathing indicates a shift in his thoughts. This varies from person to person.

After observing your friends' breathing patterns, your task is to ask them five questions each. Try to guess the answers before they respond, based on their nonverbal signals. You should do pretty well, since you've spent three days "training" them.

The Human Lie Detector

You may find that one of your friends is particularly easy to read. If that's the case, then here's another test that you can perform with him. It's both fun and revealing. In it, you'll use your sensitivity and observation skills to determine whether he is lying or telling the truth. And since you've got a "lock" on his behavior, it should be a breeze for you to be consistently accurate. Here's how you do it.

Tell your friend that you want to play a game called the Human Lie Detector. Explain that you'll ask a series of yes-or-no questions.

Ask three questions that you know he'll answer yes to. Let's say your friend is named Bob Johnson, a plumber who drives a black van. You can ask him:

Is your name Bob Johnson?
Are you a plumber?
Do you drive a black van?

Next, ask him three questions he'll answer no to. For instance:

Is your name Joe Blackman?
Are you a dentist?
Do you drive a red Ferrari?

As you've probably guessed, his responses to these questions enable you to calibrate his yes and no responses. Watch for changes in skin color, muscular tension around the lips, and breathing. Compare what you observe between his yes answers and his no answers.

Continue asking questions that you know the answers to. Switch back and forth between yes and no questions. Soon you'll begin to consistently recognize a pattern in his unconscious visible responses. When you feel that you can distinguish between his responses, begin asking questions that you don't know the answer to. Tell him that he can either lie or tell the truth.

Here are some sample questions:

Did you grow up in California?
Are you the oldest child in your family?
Do you own a tennis racquet?
Have you ever been to London?
Do you like sirloin steak?

You will notice if there is any inconsistency between his verbal answer and his physiological response. If his face tenses up in what you've observed as a no response, while he verbally answers yes, you'll know that he's lying. If his unconscious visible responses correspond with his answers, you know that he's telling the truth. By the end, your friend may be wide-eyed in disbelief. It'll appear as if you're reading his mind.

Try It in the Real World

The next step is to use your new awareness in the real world. There are dozens of opportunities to apply this skill throughout the day. Who can you do this with? Your boss, coworkers, customers, and acquaintances, for starters. Observe their unconscious visible responses and match them against your recollections. As you know, it takes a little time to observe each person before you recognize patterns.

Personally, I can't do this with casual encounters that last only a few brief moments. That's why I only perform mind-reading demonstrations with audiences near the end of my show. I read their signals during the first half, and then use that knowledge in the second half. If I haven't had a chance to properly calibrate them, my attempts to read people will fizzle.

Be patient. The extra time that it takes to learn a person's patterns will be repaid later on by accuracy.

EYE POWER

I remember receiving an e-mail after one of my magic shows. A woman from the audience was curious why I hadn't chosen her for one of the demonstrations. She wanted to know how I selected people to participate. "Are some people easier to read than others?" she asked.

As an entertainer, I have an obligation to amuse and amaze the audience. So, yes. I purposely select people who appear easier to read. There's a certain look in people's eyes that I search for. If you show me that look, the odds are higher that I'll choose you. No use wasting time on someone else who may slow the pace down.

What is that look? Simply put, I study the pupils of people's eyes. When I see people with larger pupils, I direct my important messages and funny lines to them. People with larger pupils are more responsive and more cooperative. Why is this?

Our pupils dilate when we see something we like. There have been many research studies that demonstrate this consistently. In one study, men were shown two different photographs of the same woman. However, the researchers altered her pupil size in one of the photos. The majority of men found the woman with larger pupils to be significantly more attractive. Magazine editors sometimes take advantage of this knowledge and touch up the pupil size of their cover models. Under bright studio lights, the models' pupils actually shrink during the photo shoot. In order to increase magazine sales, however, editors alter the photographs to make the models appear more desirable to newsstand browsers.

You can apply this knowledge too. Look at the pupils of people you meet. If their pupils are large when they look at you, it is a sign of approval—they like what they see. Consider this a silent form of permission. The person may be physically attracted to you, or at least interested in what you have to say. (He may, however, also be scared. When people look at you with wide pupils, they're either attracted or petrified! The context should make it clear whether it's one or the other.)

When you stand in front of a group, search out people whose eyes have the widest pupils. Their eyes offer a clear sign that they are paying attention. Play to those people and you'll receive the best responses. That's what I do, and that's how I choose my participants. I single out the most receptive people early in the show. It takes only a few to get the rest of the audience going. I aim for about a dozen people scattered throughout the room. Their laughter and enthusiasm become contagious to the rest of the group.

Yes, it's difficult to see the pupils of individuals when you're at the podium in a large auditorium. Use this technique with small to medium-size groups. And of course, one-on-one. A word of caution: don't mistakenly dismiss brown-eyed people. Sometimes it's hard to see their pupils. The contrast isn't as clear as in people with light eyes. Brown-eyed audience members may be interested in you; you just won't see it as clearly.

Pay proper attention so that you don't turn away the very people who are interested in you most.

Care for Your Own Eyes

Remember that other people are also observing *your* eyes. Unless they've read this book, though, they may not be consciously aware of their behavior. Here are some things you can do to give off the best impression to others.

· Even if you don't wear contact lenses, carry a small dropper bottle of saline solution. I keep one inside my magic case. Right before I step onstage, I apply one drop of saline to each eye. It helps make you look and feel more alert.

· Remove your glasses when you don't need them. If you do need to wear glasses, make sure the lenses have an antireflective coating. This coating prevents glare and enables others to see your pupils more clearly.

· Make sure your eyes are clear, not bloodshot. People enjoy gazing into attractive eyes.

Eye Contact

In chapter 4, "Building Confidence Before the Curtain Rises," you learned how to use your eyes to assert authority and give you greater confidence. Remember the silverback gorilla and the stare? If you tried the exercise in that chapter, you should now feel comfortable staring into people's eyes. If you haven't, go back to that section now and practice staring for one full day.

Even after practicing, you may still feel the urge to look away or shift your gaze from time to time. I have one word of advice. Don't. Eye contact increases the self-esteem of both the looker and the lookee. Each time you look away, you make the other person less sure of himself. Your relationship becomes wobbly. The simple act of holding and maintaining eye contact is the first step toward persuading people to buy into you and your ideas.

Asking questions is another way to bring people back if you notice that they're drifting. Make sure, though, that your questions require more than just a yes or no answer. It's easy for people to pretend that they're interested in something by mechanically saying "uh-huh" and gratuitously nodding their heads. Be sure to ask unspecified questions—questions that you don't know the answer to. ("What did you think of Johnson's report?" "Where are you going on your next vacation?") This type of question forces people to refocus on the present moment. They have to make a conscious effort to respond. When they feel the spotlight shining on them, you've successfully roped them back in.

Make Your Date Open Up

Here's a secret that you can use to make your date express his or her true feelings. It'll work wonders when you want to open someone up to you emotionally. Here's how it works. At the beginning of your next encounter, give your date plenty of eye contact. This makes him feel special and he'll know that you're interested. So far so good.

Later on during your date, ask a revealing question about a sensitive topic, such as commitment or marriage. Right after asking your question, quickly break eye contact and look down at your glass, or off to one side. If you're at a restaurant, focus your eyes on your plate. Whatever you do, don't look at his eyes.

He will feel that something's wrong—that he's lost his connection with you. In an act of desperation, he'll attempt to regain your attention by speaking more honestly and openly about his feelings. In general, men are more inclined to reveal their emotions when you break eye contact. Once he's opened up to you, regain your eye contact and encourage him to keep going. You've pushed him over the hurdle by making him work for your attention.

Reading Eye Movements

People are entirely unaware that they send subtle signals with their eyes. Different eye movements are linked to specific areas of thought. If you learn how to read these signals, you'll be one step closer to understanding people's thought processes. Psychotherapists Bandler and Grinder explored such "eye accessing cues" in *Frogs into Princes*, their classic book about neurolinguistic programming. As a magician, I've been applying this research to my performances for years.

You need to know three things:

1. When people concentrate on something visual, their eyes look upward.

   Up to the right = something visual that they've remembered from their past

   Up to the left = something visual that they've created in their minds

2. When people concentrate on an imaginary sound, their eyes look to the side or straight ahead.

3. When people concentrate on a feeling or sensation, their eyes look downward.

You'll be surprised at how apparent these eye movements are once you start paying attention. Yet most people have no idea that they're doing them. Here's a game you can play with a friend that's based on these findings. You'll convince your friend that you can read minds, but you'll simply be studying his eyes. Follow this script with your friend:

"IMAGINE THAT you're walking through the park. You see a bird flying. Please visualize it landing on a tree branch. Really see the bird in your mind, especially the colors on its feathers.

"Now imagine that you're standing in a large parking lot. Someone's car alarm has gone off, and it's very loud. Think of the sound this alarm is making.

"Finally, imagine that you've just eaten a slice of pizza. Recall the oil on your fingers, and how you wiped your fingers clean on a napkin.

"You're thinking of three separate experiences—the bird, the car alarm, and the oily pizza. Please concentrate on one of these experiences. Try to relive it in your mind."

STUDY HIS eyes, but don't be too obvious about it. Watch for one of the three main movements. If his eyes move up, he's thinking of the bird. If they dart to the side or stay straight, he's thinking of the car alarm. If they drop down, he's thinking of the pizza.

Reveal to your friend which item he is thinking of. He'll be impressed. You can repeat this, and it'll work again without repeating the categories.

In the real world, you can use these eye indicators to tell when someone is lying to you. If you ask someone a question and his eyes move in the expected direction, the odds are high that he responded truthfully. If his eyes move in a direction that *contradicts* his verbal response, however, you can bet he's lying. For instance, if his eyes are frozen forward when they should be looking up (while recalling something visual), his answer may be fabricated. He's trying too hard to control his own physiology.

Is this technique one hundred percent reliable? Of course not. There's no such thing as an across-the-board indicator of people's thoughts. The goal of this book, however, is to teach you to think like a magician. And magicians like to play the odds. Anything that provides you with an edge over others is worth knowing.

TRUE TALES
FROM THE MILLIONAIRES' MAGICIAN

Anecdote 6
STEVE COHEN²

I was engaged to entertain at a black-tie fund-raising event in New York's luxurious Pierre hotel. The printed program booklet listed Steve Cohen as one of the major donors, and I suddenly became confused. I hadn't donated any large sums of money. Surely there must be a mistake. After asking around, I learned that billionaire Steve Cohen, owner of SAC Capital and one of Wall Street's top traders, was in attendance that night.

We were introduced and exchanged pleasantries. He asked me to show his friends a trick. I fanned out five one-dollar bills and encouraged all of the traders to watch closely. In a split second, I transformed the bills into five hundred-dollar bills. Not a bad rate of return! The crowd was duly impressed, but the billionaire's wife was unmoved. She looked me square in the eye and said, "My Stevie does that every day of the week."

Tough crowd!

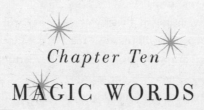

Chapter Ten

MAGIC WORDS

WITH THE CONFIDENCE-BUILDING TECHNIQUES from the previous chapters under your belt, you're well on your way to behaving like a magician. The only thing missing is some magic words.

The traditional magic words, known by all, are

- *abracadabra*—an Aramaic word that means "As I speak, I shall create,"
- *hocus-pocus*—a seventeenth-century mock-Latin word that was later contracted to the English word "hoax," and
- *presto*—Italian for "quickly," as in the way that we magicians move our fingers.

Incantations such as these were thought to invoke the mysterious forces of the universe. However, few modern audiences would believe that these words have intrinsic power. As you learned earlier in chapter 2, "Conviction: Give Them a Magic Moment," magic words are merely theatrical devices that help create a Magic Moment. When a conjuror waves his wand and says magic words, he's relying on the power of Maxim 3: Don't State—Suggest.

Magicians *do* use magic words, but in a different way than you might expect. We carefully plan out our "patter" (magic lingo for "script") so that certain points are highlighted and others deemphasized. In this chapter, you'll learn ten specific word patterns—*real* magic words—that you can systematically apply to your own life. These patterns will help you alter outcomes to your own benefit.

Once you have mastered these patterns, they will become second nature to you, and people will instantly react in predictable ways. Sounds like a creepy form of mind control, doesn't it? Fortunately, it is much simpler than that.

The basic word patterns you'll learn speak directly to the listeners' subconscious mind. I first learned of these patterns through my study of neurolinguistic programming. If you're skeptical of all that neurolinguistic programming professes to teach, no need to worry. So am I. But everything in this chapter *works*. I've used each of these language patterns in my performances for over ten years, so for those of you who doubt that any of this is possible, rest assured that these Magic Words are more than just window dressing. You'll be able to influence people more effectively once you have mastered them.

This chapter is presented in a different format from the rest of the book. I've organized it like a foreign-language phrase book. Flip to any one of the language patterns, and you'll be able to focus on two or three pages of detailed descriptions, and examples of how to use that pattern in your own life.

Collectively, these Magic Words are referred to by magicians as "linguistic deception." The term "linguistic deception" may be viewed as a euphemism for the word "manipulation." Yes, we are "manipulating" the response of our listener to fulfill our desired outcome. However, since the word "manipulation" has such negative connotations, you may further consider these techniques to be unethical or unjust. But, as you read this chapter, recognize that linguistic deception is no more sneaky or sly than the popularly used guilt trip employed by mothers and others worldwide. ("Don't bother calling me. I'll just sit here all alone by myself. In the dark. It's okay, really it is!") The linguistic deceptions that I've presented in this chapter are simply tools that you can store in your toolbox of persuasion.

Turn the page and start learning. (By the way, the sentence you just read follows Pattern 1: layered commands.)

1. LAYERED COMMANDS
"Stand up and hold this card so everyone can see it."

Imagine that you are seated in the audience at my magic show. I walk over to you, hand you the ace of spades, and say, "Stand up and hold this card so everyone can see it." Seconds later you are on your feet, displaying the ace to the group. Whether you know it or not, I've used a special pattern that forced you to follow my commands.

If I were to command you, "Stand up!" you would probably say no, or ask me why. It is natural to resist a direct command.

In the same vein, if I were to command you, "Hold this card so everyone can see it," you may feel uncomfortable agreeing. Why voluntarily be thrust into the spotlight?

Amazingly enough, when I combine these two commands "Stand up and hold this card so everyone can see it"—I am absolutely certain that you will comply. Why is that? And how can I know for sure that you will obey?

This technique is based on a simple pattern:

[Command] and [Command]

The word "and" joins the first and second commands. The listener is overwhelmed with information. He doesn't know which command to resist, so he accepts both. Just when he is about to resist the first command, he is hit with the second. It takes less effort to carry out the layered commands than to resist either one of them.

Of course, the listener does not logically work through every step that I've outlined. He processes this thought pattern quickly and subconsciously. He will not feel as if he has been manipulated. He will feel that he made the "right" choice by following your commands.

You can start using layered commands right away in a wide variety of settings.

At home:

Take out the garbage and close the door behind you.
Go upstairs and clean your room.

On a date:

Look at me and smile.
Come over here and give me a kiss.

At the office:

Call me at two o'clock and give me an update.
Finish this project and let me know when you're done.

On a Web site:

Click here and visit our site.
Contact us and ask how we can help.

Could people resist this pattern? Certainly. Do they? Of course. But in my experience, people will consistently comply. The exception is if one of the two commands is more weighted than the other. For example, don't expect too many results from the statement "Stand over there and shoot this pistol at me." The listener won't resist standing over there but will strongly resist shooting the pistol. This simple pattern will not cause the listener to do something that is against his moral base. It will, however, push someone over the edge if the two commands are reasonable.

People are more likely to carry out your layered commands when they feel that you are an authority figure. It helps if you appear strong—even a bit threatening—when you issue your commands. Try this. If you wear glasses, tilt your head forward and peer at the listener over your glasses' rims. The directness of this gaze throws the listener off guard. There is no barrier between the two of you. Even if you don't wear glasses, tilt your head forward and raise your eyes to meet your listener's. The white area below your iris should show. This gaze is intense. The combination of your facial expression and the psychological strength of this pattern will have people following your commands in no time.

2. THE TRAILING "OR"
"Would you like to shuffle the deck, or . . . ?"

Imagine that I were to present you with a deck of cards and ask you the question "Would you like to shuffle the deck?"

Your answer could obviously be yes or it could be no. I've left the outcome of this question entirely in your hands. This is fine if it doesn't matter to me whether or not the deck of cards is shuffled.

However, let us assume that I have secretly stacked a perfect blackjack hand on top of the deck, and I actually do *not* want you to shuffle the deck. By asking a different question—"Would you like to shuffle the deck, or . . . ?"—I am almost certain that your answer will be no. By simply adding the word "or" I can be almost entirely certain that I'll prevent you from shuffling the deck (and ensure that I can deal myself the winning hand later). How is this so?

As you know from playing the children's game Operator (also called Telephone), the more people who are involved in the chain of communication, the more mangled the message can become. Whenever two people speak, there are actually four points of communication taking place. Let's call the speaker and the listener Person A and Person B, respectively.

Point 1. What Person A is *thinking*
Point 2. What Person A *actually* says
Point 3. What Person B hears
Point 4. What Person B *thinks he hears*

As you can see, between Point 1 and Point 4, there is a lot of room for mis-communication. Magicians (and politicians, among others) take advantage of this breathing room and deliberately speak to Person B's mind.

In the example above, Person B *hears*, "Would you like to shuffle the deck, or . . . ," but in his mind, he *completes the sentence*. In his mind, he says, ". . . not." So his internal dialogue has just provided him with a negative answer. In the split second that he is afforded to process his answer to my question, his mind grasps hold of its most recent thought: ". . . not." With 98 percent certainty, I can confidently predict that his answer will be no.

Opportunities to use the trailing "or" occur a hundred times a day. Here are some examples:

"Would you mind if I eat the last one, or. . . . ?"
    (Likely answer: "No, go ahead!")
"Will there be a problem with that, or . . . ?"
    (Likely answer: "No, not at all.")
"Would you mind if I left a little early, or . . . ?"
    (Likely answer: "Well, if you're all finished. Sure.")

Try to keep thinking of ways that you can apply the trailing "or" to your own personal interactions. When the situations arise, you'll be ready.

It helps to shrug your shoulders and subtly shake your head no when you use this question format. The added body language will help ensure the proper response from your listener.

3. BECAUSE

The human mind is always searching for causes to each effect that we observe. If you see a sheet of paper moving along a desk all by itself, your first instinct is to look for the source of the air that is propelling it. Is there a draft coming in through the open door, or is the window open a crack? Our brains have developed this cause-and-effect response to simplify the way that we observe the world. If we simply were to observe all of the effects and not consider the causes, every moment of every day would be spent in utter wonder as to why all of these things were happening around us.

Of course, there are ways to play with this major assumption to manipulate the observer's experience. For example, two young college pranksters were visiting Yellowstone National Park and brought with them an old car steering wheel that was still attached to the steering shaft. While the spectators in the stands waited with their cameras for Old Faithful to blow, one of the practical jokers was positioned off to the side of the geyser, just out of sight of the rangers but in sight of many of the people in the stands.

When Old Faithful began to sputter, the other guy yelled out, "Let 'er rip, Bill!" His friend began spinning the wheel furiously and Old Faithful erupted into the sky. They laughed for years afterward whenever they thought about all the spectators there that day who went away thinking that Old Faithful is just a hoax.

This well-known practical joke illustrates the false connection that was planted in the minds of the spectators. By observing a supposed cause in close proximity to an effect, they convinced themselves of a meaningless connection.

How can you use this technique to your own advantage? Observe the following sentence.

"I need you to write this down because it's very important."

The sentence begins with an imperative: "I need you to write this down." This is followed by the word "because," which is then followed by the supposed reason, "it's very important."

This sentence pattern, utilizing the word "because," is extremely powerful and taps into the same cause-and-effect response described above. As long as you use the word "because" and provide a somewhat rational-sounding reason, people will do what you ask them to do in the beginning of the sentence.

The sentence **"I need you to write this down because it's very important"** is much more effective than **"I need you to write this down."**

Ironically, psycholinguistic studies have shown that the reason that is offered after the word "because" need only sound rational; it does not necessarily have to *be* rational. For example, the sentence **"I need you to write this down because I need you to write this down"** will actually out-perform the sentence "I need you to write this down"—even though there is no sound reason provided! The key here is that the listener hears that there must be some good reason (signaled by the word "because"), so the subconscious mind opens its valve for accepting the command or request that has been made.

Try this when you are at the supermarket: Ask the person who is standing in front of you, **"Would you mind if I went ahead of you because I'm in a real hurry?"** You'll find that most people will yield to your request and allow you to advance in line. For certain, this sentence is more effective than simply asking, "Would you mind if I went ahead of you?" The odds are high that you will be on your way home sooner if you use the former sentence rather than the latter.

4. LET ME TELL YOU A SECRET

When you want to make people lean in close and listen, say:

"Let me tell you a secret . . ."

or

"I shouldn't really tell you this, but . . ."

or

"Promise that you won't tell anyone about this, okay?"

Who can't resist hearing a secret? Most people like to know behind-the-scenes information about how and why things work. Preface a message with "Let me tell you a secret," and a flashing light goes off in the listener's head that signals "Pay attention." As an added dramatic touch, look quickly over your shoulder, making sure that the coast is clear, and then lean forward as you deliver the inside scoop.

As a magician, I don't advocate the release of secrets that might damage others. Rather, make your "secret" something that seems juicy but is actually just another fact that you would've released anyway.

This pattern creates a bond of intimacy. After all, we share secrets only with our closest friends. When you communicate information with the understanding that it goes "no further than this room," the other person will later reciprocate by giving something back to you. You've established that you trust that person. This sense of trust makes people think, "What a nice person. He has my best interests at heart."

In *Influence: The Psychology of Persuasion,* Robert Cialdini describes Vincent, an extraordinary waiter who made more money in tips than any other waiter in their restaurant. Cialdini took a job as a busboy at that restaurant so that he could listen in on Vincent's shtick. He followed Vincent around and learned how reciprocity played such a large role in earning bigger tips.

In general, waiters and waitresses want your bill to grow as large as possible, because the size of their tip increases too. If a waiter suggests only the most expensive items on the menu, guests may feel like they're being hustled for a larger tip.

Vincent was different. He had a routine that he used with larger groups. When one guest was ordering, he would crinkle his eyebrows, lean forward, and speak in a hushed voice so that the other tables couldn't hear. He'd say, "I'm afraid that is not as good tonight as it normally is. Might I suggest the _____ or the _____?" The two dishes he'd recommend would be cheaper than the originally selected menu item. He apparently had argued against his own best interest. But what actually happened is quite amazing. Like clockwork, patrons would tip him more generously at the end of the meal. They also trusted his recommendations for wine and dessert, which they might have otherwise turned down. After all, Victor had *saved* them money on their entrées.

If you want to get something from people, you need to give something to them first. That's the rule of reciprocity.

Now that you know how to use this secret pattern, promise you won't tell anyone else, okay?

5. SCARCITY AND THE TAKEAWAY CLOSE

The best way to make a good deal is to have the ability to walk away from it.
—*Brian Koslow*

Offer me a chocolate éclair, and I'll eat it.

Offer me a chocolate éclair, and then pull it away from me. Now I want it even more.

When you remove something that people want, they feel gypped. They want whatever has become unattainable. Scarcity makes things appear more valuable.

When I was a student at Tannen's Magic Camp, professional magician Tom Ogden explained how he handles incoming phone calls. When someone calls for a potential booking, he taught us:

1. Say, "One moment, let me check my date book."
2. Put down the phone.
3. Go make a sandwich.
4. Come back.
5. Pick up the phone and say, "Yes, I'm available that day."

If you jump quickly at someone's offer to buy from you, you appear desperate. Never appear too eager to make a sale. Ogden was clearly joking about the sandwich, but it served as a lesson, reminding us to hesitate before saying yes.

When someone is interested in hiring me to perform on a specific date, I'll often say: "You're lucky that I'm available that week. The week before I'll be performing in Las Vegas, and the week after I'll be in San Francisco."

I *do not* make these up. People can sense when you're lying. I always use the actual cities that are listed on my calendar. When they hear that you're available, potential customers will feel they're able to buy something that's clearly in great demand. They'll feel lucky that they are able to attain it.

I've learned never to act too excited about a particular sale. Save your excitement for after the call. Once you've hung up, you can jump up and down all you like. While you're making the deal, though, keep a poker face and project an image that your business will do just fine even if this one sale doesn't go through. An attitude of indifference makes people think that you have plenty of other customers who will buy from you.

The Takeaway

The next step I often use is known as the takeaway close. People are excited that they will be able to buy from you. Now present some sort of limitation that would prevent them from being able to complete the transaction. Remember the éclair? People want something even more when they're close to attaining it but it remains out of their reach.

After discussing prices on the phone, I'll often say, "I may not be the right entertainer for your event. After all, I *am* quite expensive. If you'd like me to recommend other entertainers who are less expensive, I'm happy to give you their phone numbers. They won't give you the full Steve Cohen experience, but they'll do an adequate job. The one thing I can tell you is that I may not be available on your date when you call back."

At this point, people are frothing at the mouth. They don't want something "adequate," they want something special. They sense that they may lose out on bringing me to their event, and they act on it by saying, "No, it's okay. I'll book it."

Note that this pattern won't be very effective if your pricing is completely out of someone's budget. If, however, your pricing is on the high end of their budget spectrum, it'll help push people to buy from you.

This pattern is based on a psychological principle called loss framing. People will often act more quickly and decisively when they are afraid of losing something. Which of the following is more effective?

A: "If you order by the end of the month, you'll save fifteen dollars."

B: "If you don't order today, the price will go up fifteen dollars next month."

The answer is B. Readers sense that they will be losing out on something if they don't act now. This is a typical loss frame pattern. Choice A is called a gain frame, and as you can see, it doesn't motivate readers to act right away.

Here are some examples of how you can use this pattern:

If you don't _____ , then you won't _____ .
If you're not serious about _____ , then this _____ may
    not be for you.
This may not be the right _____ for you. It's too _____ .

If you're not brave enough to try these patterns, you're losing out on a wonderful tool that will help you influence people.

Did you catch that? The last sentence is written in the exact pattern described in this section. Did it make you want to try these patterns? I hope so. You probably thought, "But I *am* brave enough!" You became slightly defensive, which made you want to prove your position to others— and you do this by doing exactly as I anticipated you would.

Note that this isn't manipulation. You're not forcing others to act against their will. They still have a choice, but you've made it more urgent.

6. THE SWEETEST SOUND
IN THE WORLD

People love the sound of their own names. It's the sweetest sound in the world. Use people's names at the beginning or end of sentences, and they'll be more receptive to your requests and suggestions. For instance:

"Do you think you could help me with this, Mark?"
"I guarantee you'll be delighted with your choice, Danielle."
"Julia, I've been waiting for the results of your project. When can I
    expect to see them?"
"Brian, why don't you call me tonight?"

In e-mails, many people neglect to use names. It really does make a difference, especially in such an impersonal, digital format, where every e-mail looks like every other one that arrives in your in-box. Simply remember to write, for example, "Dear Roman" or "Hi Alex" at the top of your e-mails. A simple gesture like this turns a generic e-mail into something inviting.

If you really want to win the crowd, work hard to improve your retention of people's names. Throughout my magic shows, I ask people's names, and then *use* those names. It does no good to ask someone's name if you aren't going to use it. One of the benefits of using a person's name is that it also helps you remember it. At the end of an event, say good-bye to each person by name: "Good night, Jen. Take care, Oscar. Hope to see you again, Debbie."

It's impressive, and it's not nearly as hard as it sounds. You can quickly learn a mnemonic system to associate names with mental pictures. For example, my name, Steve, sounds like "stove." When you look at my face, you can imagine boiling a pot of water on the stove on top of my head. When you're introduced to someone named Harry, think of "hairy," or even "Harrison Ford." Be playful with names and associate them with each person's face. Sometimes you'll come across someone with the same name as your relative or close friend. Simply associate the new person with your close friend. I usually imagine a party scene where I'd be introducing my close friend to the new person: "Jerry, this is Jerry. Jerry? Jerry." By imagining the name so many times, it comes to the forefront of your thoughts, and you'll be able to recall it much more quickly.

If this is too much work for you, forget about coming up with a system. At the very least, make a conscious effort to remember people's names when they introduce themselves. This simple step—making a conscious effort—will produce tremendous results. When you focus on something, it suddenly becomes more visible to you. This is an odd phenomenon that you've probably experienced, for instance, when buying a new car. Once you've decided to purchase a particular model, you suddenly notice many more cars on the street that are the same model as yours.

Remembering names is just the same. When you pay attention (that's the key!), remembering names is not nearly as hard as you first imagined. Rather, it becomes quite simple.

Use names, dear reader, and people will listen to you with greater interest.

7. DON'T READ THIS SECTION
"Stop. Don't read any further.
You don't want to learn this technique."

With a heading like that, you're compelled to read this section even more. Why?

Our minds think in positive images. The word "don't" means nothing to our subconscious. When you read the heading above, you instinctively think, "Read this section." Then your conscious mind steps in and negates that positive image.

When you hear:	*You first think:*
Don't do that.	Do that.
Don't feel afraid.	Feel afraid.
Don't step on my toes.	Step on my toes.

We all think in pictures, and there's no such thing as a negative picture. Of course, people have created symbols that mean "don't," such as a large X or a red circle with a slash through it. But these symbols can only be applied after you've first concentrated on what it is you want to negate.

Throughout our childhood, we're told, "Don't do this, don't do that." Unfortunately for parents, the word "don't" is heard so much that it is ignored, serving as an invitation to actually perform the undesirable behavior! Especially with children, but even with adults, it's better to say what you want, as opposed to what you don't want. For instance:

Change this sentence:	To this sentence:
Don't forget to bring your keys.	Remember to bring your keys.
Don't worry about it.	Everything is under control.
Don't drop that.	Carry that carefully.
Don't forget to call me.	Remember to call me, okay?

When you give directions to groups of people, it's always better to speak directly so that they understand your directions clearly. During my shows, I ask each audience member to fold an index card in half. Unintentionally, I used to confuse people by speaking in the negative, "Don't fold it the long way, fold it the short way." Now I speak more precisely, saying, "Fold your card in half so the writing is on the inside. After you've made your fold, the card should look like this." I hold up a sample folded card so that people can confirm that they've followed the directions properly. This simple change in wording, along with a visual aid, eliminated a previously awkward moment in the show.

I saved the best part for last. Now that you know that the word "don't" plants the opposite thought in people's minds, you can purposely use this to your advantage. Instead of the positive-not-negative tactic you already learned, this time you'll actually use the word "don't" to influence the direction of people's thoughts.

Here's the pattern:

Don't _____ unless _____ .

For instance:

"Don't consider buying this unless you're absolutely sure."
"Don't read this report unless you really want to impress the boss."
"Don't decide now unless it feels right to you."
"Don't say yes unless you mean it."

Can you feel how strongly the opposite meaning is expressed in each of these sentences? When you use the word "don't," people think, "Why not?" Their curiosity is heightened until you provide some justification for them to follow your command. The justification comes after the word "unless," and this information is usually something desirable to the listener.

Don't bother learning this pattern unless you are serious about persuading people. (Catch that?) Write out five sentences that follow this pattern and you'll be on your way to becoming a master influencer. And please, don't read the rest of this book.

8. ASSUMING THE OBVIOUS
"You probably know this already."

As I'm sure you know, people don't like to admit that they aren't aware of important things. They'll pretend that they know what you're talking about, simply to avoid looking ignorant. You realize, of course, that this tendency makes people more likely to believe the statements you make. After all, they have no information available to refute what they've heard.

If you believe what you read in the previous paragraph, you've already been ensnared by the next technique—assuming the obvious. Reread the last paragraph and look at the words starting the sentences:

"As I'm sure you know . . . "
"You realize, of course . . . "
"After all . . . "

These lead-ins assume that the listener considers the following statement to be *obvious information*. Most people will not interrupt you to say, "No, I wasn't aware of that" or "No, I didn't realize this." Speak with confidence, and the statements that follow this type of lead-in will sound extremely believable.

Here are some alternative lead-ins:

"You probably already know that . . ."

"I'm sure you realize . . ."

"You must've heard that . . ."

Clearly, you can't use this technique to make an entirely outlandish statement. Nobody will believe you if you say, "You probably already know that alien spacecrafts landed on my roof this morning." The only thing they *will* believe is that you need professional help. Use this technique to emphasize something that's believable, something you don't think people would question. Assuming the obvious helps make you sound like an authority. It is even more effective when you act like an authority—speak sincerely and confidently, and keep your gaze intent. Don't flinch or shift your eyes off to the side. A confident demeanor helps sell your words even more. But I'm sure you already knew that.

9. QUALIFIERS
"How soon will you start using this pattern?"

I use this subtle and diabolical technique all the time. The key to using qualifiers is the word "how." Above, the subtitle asks: **"How soon will you start using this pattern?"** Let's examine this sentence. If I had asked, "Will you start using this pattern?" you could reply with a simple yes or no. But because the question began with the words "How soon . . . ," you focus on something entirely different. Instead of pondering whether or not you'll use this pattern, you concentrated on *when* you'd start using it.

This pattern presumes, or presupposes, that what follows later in the sentence is true. In presenting the question this way, I've forced you to imagine yourself actually using this pattern. It's not a matter of *if*, it's a matter of *when*.

Here are some examples of how easy it is to use qualifiers:

"How impressed will you be with this?"

(Instead of saying, "Will you be impressed with this?" you've pre-supposed that he'll be impressed. Now it's just a matter of degree. Will he be somewhat impressed, very impressed, or extremely im-pressed? Regardless, you've set the other person up to be im-pressed.)

"How quickly can you clean your room?"

(I use this with my son all the time, instead of asking, "Would you clean your room?" It's amazing how quickly he jumps to it.)

"Are you curious about how my company can help promote your event?"

(Instead of saying, "Did you know that my company can help pro-mote your event?" you've presupposed that your company can in-deed promote the event. You've shifted attention to *whether or not the listener is curious* about how you'll do it.)

"Let me ask you how serious you are about purchasing this."

(Instead of saying, "Are you serious about purchasing this?" you force the listener to evaluate his degree of commitment. You've presupposed that he'll buy from you. You just want to know whether he's serious enough to buy today, or if he's still in the just-looking stage.)

There are dozens more examples that you can create yourself. Simply in-sert an adjective or adverb after the word "how" and you'll be on your way. Here are some more examples:

"How relaxed will you be when . . . ?"
"How comfortable will you feel when . . . ?"
"How soon will you use your new . . . ?"
"How surprised will you be when . . . ?"

I particularly enjoy using the last one, because it presupposes that people will be surprised. In my performances I often ask, "How surprised will you be when the coin . . . disappears?" I let this question hang in a rhetorical fashion. I don't push the audience to verbally respond. People answer the question silently in their minds, and then truly become very surprised when the coin does indeed vanish at my fingertips. For your information, and hopefully to inspire you to try this pattern, audience reactions have increased dramatically ever since I began adding this simple line right before the magic occurs.

How excited are you about using this new pattern? Try it out for yourself and see.

10. EITHER/OR QUESTIONS

During seventeenth-century witch hunts, women suspected of practicing witchcraft were strapped to a chair (called a ducking stool) and submerged into a river. If a woman drowned, this proved that she was mortal, and not a witch. If she survived, however, this was proof that she possessed supernatural powers, and she was sentenced to execution. As you can see, the poor woman died either way.

Circular reasoning such as this offers people an illusion of choice. Psychologists call this the double bind—you're damned if you do, and you're damned if you don't. The double bind was formulated in the 1950s by Gregory Bateson and studied extensively by Milton Erickson for his use in hypnotherapy sessions. Erickson would ask patients, **"Would you be more comfortable going into a trance in this chair or that chair?"** Whichever chair they chose, patients accepted that they would indeed go into a trance. It was just a matter of *where*.

This format has been applied to sales in the "alternate advance" close, described by Tom Hopkins in his classic book *How to Master the Art of Selling*. Instead of asking a customer, "Are you interested in buying this sofa?" the clever salesman asks: **"Which delivery date is best for you, the first or the fifteenth?"** When the customer replies, "I need it by the first," he's basically saying, "Yes, I'll buy this sofa from you." This pattern assumes that the sale is already a fait accompli. Now it's just a matter of determining *when* the item will be delivered.

Instead of making people answer yes/no questions, get them to answer a "W" question: who, what, where, when, why. These types of questions help tide you past resistance. In your "W" question, include two options so that the listener can choose an outcome.

Instead of:	"Do you want to eat out tonight?"
Ask:	"Which restaurant do you want to eat at tonight, Golden Unicorn or Key Palace?"
Instead of:	"Do you want to do something this weekend?"
Ask:	"When do you want to go into the city with me, on Saturday or Sunday?"
Instead of:	"How come you never get your projects in on time?"
Ask:	"When will I have your project on my desk, Friday afternoon or Monday morning?"
Instead of:	"Would it be all right for me to come over to your office sometime?"
Ask:	"I'll be near your office today. Which time would be more convenient for me to stop in, two o'clock or three-thirty?

As you can see, the second question in each pair makes an assumption. When someone answers the question, they can only function within the framework of that assumption. The key is to offer two options, both of which assume that you will move ahead.

Don't you agree that this form of communication is more effective? It skips past the natural instinct that most people have—the no instinct. It's easy for people to answer no and shoot everything down. You want to avoid giving them that option. That's why you might want to consider using either/or questions. This pattern encourages people to provide more substantial answers.

TIME TO PRACTICE

Now that you've read through the Magic Words in this chapter, you may be shrugging to yourself: "But I already use those phrases . . ." That's right, you already *do* use them. We all do. They are part of everyday language. We just don't realize how powerful they are. When you decide to strategically use Magic Words in your daily conversations, you'll be delightfully surprised at how reliably you can predict others' responses.

Remember, you are not attempting to force people to do things against their will. You're merely *influencing* them. As you practice using Magic Words, they'll become second nature to you, and you'll be dropping them into your conversations—both at work and at home. For businesspeople, these techniques can help you set the mood for positive business transactions. And for spouses, Magic Words can help you convince your partner to go along with your ideas and desires (unless both of you have read this book, of course!).

Learn the patterns and, most important, experiment with them. I think you will find yourself pleasantly surprised at how well they work.

Chapter Eleven
MISDIRECTION

To misdirect attention is to control attention.
—*Fred Robinson, British magician*

OF ALL THE SECRETS in this book, the one revealed in this chapter is the most dear to magicians. This secret is the cornerstone of my professional performances. I wasn't going to include it because I thought it was too good to give up.

However, this secret is based on published psychological principles. You have every right to learn it too.

The secret you'll be learning is misdirection. In this chapter, you'll learn what it is, what it isn't, and how you can apply it to your life.

Once you learn about misdirection, will you automatically be able to see through every magician's act? Not a chance. The principles are so compelling that you won't even recognize them when you see them. It's very difficult to consciously fight misdirection, since it is based on human nature. I know that if you hear a loud bang behind you, you're going to turn toward it. Misdirection is just like that. It won't always be that obvious, but it will be that reliable.

A QUICK EXAMPLE

Let's play a game. As quickly as you can, answer the following questions:

1. How many fingers does one man have on his hands?
2. How many fingers on ten hands?

If you're like most people, you answered "ten" and "one hundred." The first answer is correct. The second answer is wrong. Go back and read it again.

This simple example shows how misdirection works in a nutshell. The first question leads you down a particular path and puts you in a certain state of mind. When you arrive at the second question, you base your answer on your answer to the first question. Ten times ten equals one hundred. Seems simple. And that's what misdirection is. Simple. On the receiving end, it seems so harmless. *So easy*. Nevertheless, by the time you reach the finish line, you've missed out on some information along the way.

By the way, the second answer in the above game is "fifty."

GENERATIONS OF MISDIRECTION

The misdirection techniques I learned when I first started conjuring have served me for the past twenty-five years and will endure as long as magicians walk onstage. In fact, these techniques may be traced back to one of the original magic tricks—the Cups and Balls—which was performed in Egypt over four thousand years ago.

The Cups and Balls involves the vanishing, transposing, and producing of small balls from under three cups. The skillful performer of this trick is capable of making audiences look away from his secret maneuvers at just the right moment so that they never see how the balls return to each cup.

The surprising finale of this trick is usually the production of three large items, such as potatoes, billiard balls, or even live baby chicks. Audiences are delighted by this finale because they know that the magician somehow introduced those "final loads" into the cups, despite the fact that they were completely unable to see it happen. The loads were indeed openly inserted into the cups right in front of their eyes, but the audience just couldn't see it. By providing something interesting at each stage of the routine, the audience has no choice but to follow along, concentrating their attention where the magician wants them to look, and away from each of the final loads.

The misdirection used by the Egyptian conjurors still works today on modern audiences. Isn't that amazing? Despite many advances in technology and material construction, the basic psychological tenets of magic have remained unchanged for generations.

If you've ever watched Las Vegas magicians Penn and Teller perform the Cups and Balls, then you've seen how misdirection works. They use *clear plastic cups* so that you can view when and how they secretly load the balls. It's both comical and amazing. You can see the balls "secretly" coming and going, but your mind can't keep up with it. Intellectually, you know you're being distracted, but their timing is so precise that you are still baffled. Some magicians have complained that Penn and Teller have damaged the art of magic by exposing the Cups and Balls. I think that's hogwash. Their performance of this trick illustrates the fact that misdirection, when executed well, is bulletproof. Even when people *know* that they are going to be misdirected, they have no choice but to follow the magician's lead.

WORD OF CAUTION

Magicians use misdirection to trick people, but it's all in the name of fun. Unless you are interested in performing magic yourself, it's probably best not to trick people. Honesty is the best policy. Once you learn how misdirection works, I advise you to use your knowledge only for the powers of good.

TERMINOLOGY

We talk of misdirection, but this term itself is inaccurate. As a magician, I am not aiming to divert your attention *away* from a certain action, I am striving to direct your attention *toward* something else. At the beginning of this chapter, you read a quote by magician Fred Robinson: "To misdirect attention is to control attention." If you learn one thing from this chapter, let it be this point. Misdirection is not about distraction, it is about constantly controlling what the audience is thinking at each moment.

We magicians lead people to look precisely where we want them to, directing them toward—not away from—a focal point of interest. The best way to illustrate this is for me to teach you a beginner's magic trick that you can learn with a little practice. It is based entirely on misdirection.

THe VaNISHING PeN CaP

Take a pen and place the cap in the open palm of your left hand. Turn your body about three-quarters away from your audience, showing them your left shoulder.

Say, "Here we go, I'm going to make the cap disappear at the count of three. Listen and keep your eyes on the pen cap."

Brandish the pen like a magic wand in your right hand, as shown in figure 6. Tap the cap with each count of "One, two, three." Raise the pen to eye level before each tap.

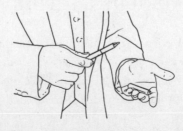

FIGURE 6.

As you bring the pen upward before tapping the third time, slip it behind your right ear and leave it there, as shown in figure 7. Observers won't notice that you've done anything tricky, because their attention will be on the pen cap. Work on the timing, because you don't want to fumble here.

FIGURE 7.

When you bring the pen down for the third tap, say, "Three." The pen will be gone from your right hand, as shown in figure 8. Make a joke: "Oh, the trick backfired. The *pen* disappeared, not the cap. I can't believe it."

FIGURE 8.

Wait a few moments to let the surprise sink in. Then turn toward the audience to reveal the pen, which has appeared magically behind your ear. The trick is over.

BONUS TRICK

Here's a follow-up trick you can do to make the cap disappear (hence the title of the trick). It continues right on the heels of the first trick that you just finished.

Close your left fist around the cap. Say, "Now I'm going to do it right. I'll make the cap vanish with this pen up here." Use your right hand to point at the pen still behind your right ear. While observers are focused on the pen, quickly place the cap in your left pocket.

Even after you've "gone south" with the pen cap (that means "gotten rid of" in magic lingo), continue to hold your left hand in a loose fist. Pretend that the cap is still inside.

Take the pen with your right hand and tap your left fist while counting to three. Open your left fist to reveal an empty palm. The pen cap has really disappeared, and nobody has a clue to where. The misdirection is so strong that audiences will see only what you direct them to see.

EVERY TEN SECONDS

As you can see from the preceding description, magicians work out tricks in painstaking detail. A casual brush of the hand or turn of the body might actually have taken months to perfect. We guide your eyes to follow a predetermined path so that you don't look at the wrong place at the wrong time. This requires a great deal of planning.

When I design a presentation for a trick, I strive to introduce new visual information every ten seconds. That's the same formula that television producers follow to prevent audiences from changing the channel. Attention spans have plummeted in recent years and television is the main culprit. The next time you watch an entertainment or news program, count to ten in your mind. When you reach ten, notice how the scene changes visually. Start counting again and you'll find that the scene changes again ten seconds later.

John Ramsey, a famous magician from Scotland, said that if you want someone to look at something, you should look at it yourself. People will pay attention to things that appear to be important. If you look at something, others will consider it worthy of their attention too.

When you are planning a presentation, spend extra time thinking about what you want your audience to be thinking about each moment. Pretend that everyone is wearing baseball caps that say "10 Seconds, Buddy," since that's all the time they'll give you before their minds drift elsewhere! Typically, speakers leave their PowerPoint slides static on the screen for minutes at a time. That's why so many audiences fade during those speakers' talks.

If you can't find something interesting to present every ten seconds, don't worry. Comedians aim for a big laugh every thirty seconds. Try that instead. Every time you stand in front of a group, think of yourself as an entertainer. You don't have to be funny. You don't have to be magical. Just be interesting.

EYES FOLLOW MOVING OBJECTS

One way to stay interesting is to keep moving. People's eyes follow movement. They have no choice. It's a survival mechanism that has helped protect humans from animal attacks and other danger since prehistoric times. Fortunately, this helps make magic performances more deceptive too.

Magicians often speak of this principle by saying "the larger action covers the smaller action." If two objects are in motion, the human eye is naturally drawn to the faster and broader of the two actions.

Magicians aren't the only people who use this principle. It's ingrained in human behavior. Basketball players, for instance, give a head fake in one direction and pass the ball in the other. Martial artists distract their opponents with a sharp upward movement, and then attack with a low kick to the abdomen. And parents most certainly use this principle with small children. If you have kids, think of how many times you've distracted them with a moving object such as a toy or a colorful ball. As soon as the child looks away, you remove something you don't want them to play with, like a pair of scissors nearby. Works every time.

Add movement to your next meeting or speech. Here are some ideas that will keep people's attention on you.

· Stand up suddenly from your chair and give the next point while standing.

· Move around the room, stopping to lean on different pieces of furniture while delivering key points. Think Phil Donohue.

· Toss objects into the audience. I saw one company president use this technique during a speech to build interest among his employees. Throughout the speech, he used a baseball bat to hit Wiffle balls into the audience. Whoever caught a ball was asked to participate in a special project that weekend. The employees' interest level was at a peak every time he pulled out the bat.

· "Accidentally" drop something—a chart, a book, some keys. People cannot help paying attention to a bang or jingle. If their minds were drifting, this will help pull them back.

· Ask people to stand up and move around the room. Any act of movement revitalizes people and interests them in what you are saying. During my show, I ask the entire audience to walk around several times. When they return to their seats, they are even more attentive.

If curiosity kills the cat, then monotony kills an audience. Remember to capture people's interest by including movement in all you do.

THE OFFBEAT

If you've ever played music, you may be familiar with syncopation. That's when the tune places emphasis on the offbeat. If a typical rhythm goes "one-and-two-and-three-and-four," the offbeat is indicated by the word "and." It's not when you tap your toe down but the moment you lift your toe up.

You probably felt the offbeat the last time you watched a horror movie. Here's a typical pattern in that genre. Tension builds with a crescendo of violins. The hero peeks through a keyhole, looking to see who's in the next room. He opens the door, walks in, and then . . . nothing happens. The violins stop, and the room is empty. "Ahhh," you sigh in relief. The moment you relax, though, a killer leaps in from behind and attacks the hero with a chain saw. *"Ahhh!"* you scream. Movie directors introduce scary episodes like this when the audience is least expecting it. They wait for the offbeat.

Magicians *live* in the offbeat. (We don't leap into rooms with chain saws, though.) We wait until the moment that tension is released. Audiences let their guard down for a split second. Only then does the magician make his move.

Since you're not a magician, you have no need to do anything sneaky during the offbeat in your own presentations. Instead, you can use the offbeat to stay several steps ahead of your audience. Use the offbeat to cinch up extra time. Allow me to explain.

When you tell a joke, everyone laughs at the punch line—assuming it's funny. They feel tension during the buildup, and relief when it's over. At the end of a joke, the audience's guard is down, since it's impossible for people to laugh and be focused at the same time. (Try it and you'll see what I mean.) But since you were the purveyor of humor, you don't laugh at your own joke. And you shouldn't. Instead, use that time to think of the next thing you'll say. Comedians wait until you're laughing before they "goose" the joke with a second, bigger laugh. They don't allow their own minds to shut down. Instead, they stay several steps ahead of the audience, thinking about how to best deliver the next jokes.

Remember: there is no need for *you* to relax. Or laugh. Or sigh. You are in complete control. The person creating the offbeat is not subject to the lack of clarity that the offbeat creates.

Acknowledge that people will feel tension when you present your ideas to them. And factor the release of that tension into your presentation. That's what the pros do. For instance, I know exactly how many seconds of applause I'll receive after each trick. This knowledge is useful, because it means I know how soon the audience will begin to pay attention again.

Early in their career, magicians Siegfried and Roy were contracted for a twenty-minute spot at the MGM Grand in Las Vegas. During rehearsals, they only performed a fifteen-minute act. The producers liked what they saw but complained that the act was too short. Roy countered by saying, "Ah, but we've factored in five minutes of applause."

When audiences laugh or applaud, your mind should be racing. They've handed you a present called "gained time" that you can use to figure out your battle plan. Remember: never relax together with your audience. You are not one of them. You are their leader and must direct them to the next point of interest.

THE DISCIPLINE OF MISDIRECTION

Misdirection is not an isolated tool. You can't stick it in a bottle and sell it. Rather, misdirection is woven into the very fabric of a magic performance. Magicians carefully place innocent-seeming jokes and gestures into performances so that audiences will relax their attention at just the right time. It's during this moment of relaxation that the magician performs his secret move to make the trick work.

Misdirection works reliably because it's been carefully thought out. You'll never have to slip potatoes or billiard balls under cups, like a magician. But you can benefit from applying the *discipline* of misdirection. Think hard about how to control your audience's attention each moment. You can't influence people who aren't paying attention. Give them cause to follow your lead by presenting something interesting at regular intervals and guiding them in the direction you desire.

Afterword

WIN THE CROWD

WHEN YOU STARTED READING this book, you may have thought, "How is a magician going to teach me to become more commanding and charismatic? Will I need to buy a magic wand? A wizard's cap? Will he teach me to zap lightning bolts out of my eyes?"

As you've progressed through the chapters, though, you've hopefully realized that the skills of a magician overlap with those of anyone who is an excellent communicator. You don't have to devote hundreds of hours to learning sleight-of-hand tricks. Instead, you need to focus on being genuine and presenting yourself as a showman. This book has provided you with many lessons that teach you to do just that. When you apply what you've learned, people will inch forward in their seats. They won't shift their attention, because they won't want to miss what you might say next.

I've presented you with my pet secrets; now it's your turn to get out and apply them. Remember PP (People Practice)? You'll only get good at winning crowds when you put yourself in scenarios where they exist. Eradicate the word "shy" from your vocabulary. Get out there and be bold. Speak with lively language, walk with a confident gait, and deliver your material with a twinkle in your eyes.

And guess what—whether you realize it or not, you're already a magician. Although you may be hard-pressed to come up with your favorite method for vanishing a handkerchief or levitating a Ferrari, you're capable of performing *real* magic. What is real magic? Simple things, like making a child smile, or helping a friend overcome an obstacle.

The powers of a magician may seem trivial on the surface, but the implications of those powers are mighty. Producing a pigeon from an empty scarf is an act of *creation*. You can create a new relationship, or a new business. You can write a book, build a house, design an exciting future. You can find opportunity where others have not before.

We all need magic in our lives—especially in times like these when there's so much uncertainty in the world. We need the feeling of wonder and mystery. Magic is a metaphor for all of the wonderful things around us. It reminds us that maybe, just around the corner, there's something that will make our lives better.

Constantly think about ways you can bring joy into other people's lives. Keep a playful spirit in all your interactions with others. That is one of the primary goals of the magician. Play your way through life. You don't need any special training. You already have the power to overcome adversity, to create, and to empower. After all, that is really what magic is all about.

FURTHER READING

Most magic books written for professional magicians are difficult to read because they're laden with industry jargon. As a nonmagician, you'd probably panic if you were suddenly instructed to "control the selected card using a Stroboscopic Riffle Pass." Sounds like heart surgery, doesn't it? The following list contains books that are much more accessible to those interested in the subjects of magic, persuasion, and personal influence. You'd certainly profit from reading any of them.

Anderson, George B. *Magic Digest: Fun Magic for Everyone*. Northfield, Ill.: DBI Books, 1972.

One of my favorite beginner magic books. Although it's been out of print for ages, you can find used copies relatively easily on the Internet. A great introduction to hundreds of tricks that require no special apparatus—just simple, common objects that are found anywhere. I refer to this book constantly to learn new tricks for my professional use. Just goes to prove that showmanship can make even the simplest trick into a big number. Track this book down. You'll also learn a lot about the history of magic from the gallery of legendary magicians, including Houdini, Okito, Kellar, Blackstone, and Thurston.

Cialdini, Robert B. *Influence: The Psychology of Persuasion*. New York: William Morrow and Co., 1993.

Darned if the author's name—Cialdini—doesn't make him sound as if he's a legendary magician too! (He's not.) *Influence* teaches six psychological secrets that marketers use to compel you to buy things, time after time. If you are in sales or marketing, this book is a must. If you're a consumer, this book will open your eyes to how master marketers persuade you to buy their wares. Fortunately, it also teaches how to protect yourself from being a patsy. In *Win the Crowd*, I introduce the concept of reciprocity. That's just one of the six secrets explained in Cialdini's classic. The others are commitment and consistency, social proof, liking, authority, and scarcity. You'll wish that you read this book when you were younger.

Greene, Robert. *The 48 Laws of Power*. New York: Penguin Putnam, 1998.

A beautifully designed book that I return to again and again. You'll learn how famous figures throughout history—including showmen P. T. Barnum and Harry Houdini—controlled the heartstrings of the masses who adored them. Hundreds of detailed stories are followed with practicable laws that you can extrapolate (with thought) to become more powerful in your business life. Like Machiavelli's prince, you'll consider it a compliment the next time someone calls you ruthless.

Hay, Henry. *The Amateur Magician's Handbook*. New York: Signet, 1974.

Here is another beginner's magic book that I refer to constantly. If this book doesn't make you want to become a magician, then nothing will. Hay wrote *Handbook* with passion—teaching challenging manipulation techniques alongside essays that analyze how to *really* entertain modern audiences. I grew up reading this book as a child, lost it, then found it again and rejoiced in reading it all over, from cover to cover.

Levy, Benjamin. *Remember Every Name Every Time*. New York: Fireside, 2002.

The appendix of this book is priceless—a list of the top forty most popular first names in America, and how to memorize them. Simply link the mnemonic provided with prominent features on the faces of people you meet, and you'll soon look like a memory expert. Other authors, including magician and memory expert Harry Lorayne, have written books on remembering names, but I've found this one particularly helpful, especially with its full-color photo practice pages.

Nelms, Henning. *Magic and Showmanship: A Handbook for Conjurers*. New York: Dover Publications, 1969.

All of the top magicians have studied this book cover to cover. Most magic books focus on the tricks, but this one focuses on how to *present* those tricks. That's the real secret of magic. Nelms was a stage director and applied his understanding of the theater to magicians. Contains the classic story of adding meaning to magic: If a magician asked you to put your hand into your pocket and you pulled out a ham sandwich, that would be a pretty good trick. After your initial surprise, though, your only feeling would be, "So what?" However, if you were to first say, "I'm hungry," and then the magician asked you to put your hand into your pocket, where you found that same ham sandwich, you'd consider it a miracle. The trick suddenly makes sense because it answers a need. It arises out of the context of the situation. Read this book for its explanations of controlling attention (chapter 14) and the interest curve (chapter 18). These lessons apply to anyone—with a magic wand or without—who plans to win an audience.

Pratkanis, Anthony, and Elliot Aronson. *Age of Propaganda*. New York: W. H. Freeman and Co., 2001.

While this book presents dozens of examples of how media and businesses have abused the power of persuasion, you will also learn just as many ways to subtly use those techniques to your advantage. While this is not a how-to book, you'll be able to easily apply these lessons with a little thought.

Reis, Al. *Focus: The Future of Your Company Depends on It*. New York: HarperCollins Publishers, 1996.

I "became" the Millionaires' Magician after reading this book. (Read about this transition in chapter 3 of *Win the Crowd*.) Reis claims, "The sharper your knife, the better it cuts." This means that you'll obtain better results when you pool your efforts into one area. This book is valuable for CEOs and marketers who want to hone a company or brand, but also (with some thought) for people who find themselves floundering in their interests. Focus your immediate attention on improving specific areas of your life, until you have them mastered.

Schwartz, David J. *The Magic of Thinking Big*. New York: Simon & Schuster, 1987.

I must admit that I was first drawn to this self-help book because it had the word "magic" in the title. A casual flip-through, however, forced me to realize that this was worth much more careful study. This book, which has sold over 4 million copies, is a dynamo in its field. If you want to learn how to think like a leader, overcome insecurity, and achieve your deepest goals in life, go out and buy this book immediately. I've given dozens of copies of this book to my friends and loved ones.

Silverman, Kenneth. *Houdini!!! The Career of Erich Weiss.* New York: Harper-Collins Publishers, 1996.

If you like biographies that read like novels, this is the book for you. Although Houdini was not considered to be a very good magician by his peers (plenty of magicians were proud that they had "fooled Houdini"), nobody would deny that he was a master showman and clever self-promoter who we still remember to this day. This is the most thoroughly researched history of Harry Houdini's life ever printed, and you'll find it fascinating.

ACKNOWLEDGMENTS

First and foremost, thank you to my wife, Yumi, and our children, Alex and June. Your love and companionship are the true magic in my life.

I kneel down in reverence to Mark Levy. I feel blessed that I've found the perfect friend.

Thank you to one of my biggest secrets: Jennifer Joel at ICM. She does magic, too. With a wave of her wand (and a few phone calls), Jennifer magically turned me into an author.

Thank you to my parents, Elaine and Jay Cohen, for chauffeuring me as a young magician from show to show before I could drive.

Thank you to Holly Peppe for mentoring me while still finding time to save the world.

Chamber Magic thanks to Eric Long, Mark Lauer, Shelley Clark, and all of my colleagues at The Waldorf-Astoria hotel. Also, Matthew Martinucci, Catherine Woodd, Hossein Vetry, and Miyoko Kawashima at the Ritz-Carlton San Francisco. It is an honor to work with you all.

Thank you to those who contributed material to this book: Brian Cohen, Bob Dagger, Samantha Ettus, Rett Foster, David Friedman, Yuki Kadoya, Julia Kaye, David Levine, Scott Livingston, Brian Zachary Mayer, Nicky McAllister, Lisa Menna, and Jay Sabatino. In addition to the many magicians quoted throughout the text, I am also indebted to Juan Tamariz, Paul Harris, Kenton Knepper, Eugene Burger, Tommy Wonder, and my delightful friend Derren Brown.

Finally, thank you to my editor, Matthew Benjamin, and the entire staff at HarperCollins. Your faith in my work is most appreciated.

INDEX

ABOUT THE AUTHOR

Among high society and the sophisticated set, Steve Cohen is known as The Millionaires' Magician. His demonstrations of magic and mind reading have baffled some of the world's most successful people, including David Rockefeller, Jack Welch, Carl Sagan, and Michael Bloomberg.

After learning his first trick at age six, Cohen was hooked. When his uncle Nat Zuckerman made a Morgan silver dollar disappear, it vanished in a puff of smoke. Just like Merlin! At the time, Cohen thought that this was real magic. He did not realize until he was older that all of his relatives smoked cigarettes, and the entire room was full of tobacco smoke.

The magical atmosphere made quite an impression on his young mind. At every family gathering, he cornered Uncle Nat and asked him to repeat the same tricks over and over again. The two of them—master and pupil—spent hours refining difficult card manipulation techniques, and Cohen fondly remembers the day when his uncle said, "The student has surpassed the teacher. You're on your own now." Cohen accepted the challenge and has made magic his life.

Throughout his adolescence, Cohen spent much time studying professional-level magic books. Every summer vacation, the Cohen family drove around the United States in an RV. (They'd explored all fifty states by the time that Steve turned ten years old.) In each city, Steve opened the Yellow Pages and called up local magicians so that they could spend time together "talking shop." Old men

182 ABOUT THE AUTHOR

met with the young student, passing on tips and tricks that they had learned through years of experience in the trenches.

The magic fraternity is run like a meritocracy; magicians are more forthcoming with information when they see that somebody new is bringing genuine interest to the table, not just a desire to learn "secrets." By the end of high school, many of Cohen's best friends were professional magicians located in Ohio, California, Texas, and New York City. They formed a close bond that included sharing techniques known only to the inner circle. His parents allowed him to travel alone to visit his friends around the country, and Cohen was often fond of saying that he had more frequent-flier miles than any of his schoolmates.

Today, Cohen continues to travel, though now for corporate and private engagements. When he is not on the road, he can be found at New York's famous Waldorf-Astoria hotel performing his public show, *Chamber Magic.* Cohen recreates the intimacy of nineteenth-century parlor performances by baffling his guests in the close quarters of a private suite. *Chamber Magic* has been running continuously at The Waldorf Towers for four years and has enjoyed further sold-out successes in London's West End and at San Francisco's Ritz-Carlton hotel.

He has performed at a wide variety of gatherings, from the White House Correspondents Dinner to Fortune 500 corporate events and private functions.

Cohen has received widespread recognition from the media, including CNN, *Martha Stewart Living, CBS Evening News, The Early Show,* CNNfn, the *History Channel,* the *New York Times,* the *Financial Times,* the *New York Post, Lexus Magazine,* the *Sunday Times* London, and the *Evening Standard.*

Cohen earned a degree in psychology from Cornell University and spent a year abroad studying at Waseda University in Tokyo. He has native-level proficiency in Japanese and previously worked as an interpreter for the Japanese government. He holds the esteemed rank of MIMC (Member of the Inner Magic Circle) with Gold Star, awarded by The Magic Circle in London.

He lives in New York City with his wife and their two children.

For information on a live
STEVE COHEN MAGIC PERFORMANCE
at your company or private event, visit:

www.chambermagic.com

"You've got to see this magician. He's terrific."

—Michael Bloomberg, mayor of New York City

"Steve managed to entrance, mystify, and totally entertain one of the wealthiest and demanding of audiences for several hours. I was so mesmerized that I hired him on the spot to entertain at my law firm's annual party two weeks later."

—Robert Mittman, Esq.

"Steve captivated a room of two hundred GM employees and held them all spellbound even our most skeptical executives!"

—Jim Kraus, General Motors

"I was happy to be reminded of the Rockefeller family luncheon party when Steve performed so wonderfully for all of our guests. I know that they were all thrilled."

—Mrs. David Rockefeller

"How did he know the words that had just gone through my head? Steve Cohen does things that you simply can't believe."

—Gersh Kuntzman, New York Post